## MEET THE GREAT QUARTERBACKS

**STABLER:** "I don't set personal goals, like number of completions, touchdown passes, and other things like that. The only goal any player should have is to win. And the ultimate win is the Super Bowl. That's what I want. Because if I'm the quarterback of the team that wins the Super Bowl, then evidently I did something right along the way."

**KILMER:** "I'm sure I fell asleep at the wheel. The car went off the road and began plunging into the ditch. My right leg got caught under the brake pedal. I could feel it snap, and I could see the bone coming through. . . . I had to look at it this way. My life was athletics and I figured I was too young to give it all up. Nobody ever came out and said I *couldn't* play football any more. They just said they didn't think I would. Well, I had to find out for myself whether I could or I couldn't."

**BRADSHAW:** "I was happy to be chosen by the Steelers. I wanted to go to a losing team all along. That way, if the team became a winner they'd do it with me. From the first time I went to Pittsburgh and met some of the guys and the coaches, I knew the Steelers were a team in search of a leader. That's what I'm going to be paid for . . . to be a leader."

**STAUBACH:** "I'm confident in myself. I know I won't be number one immediately, but I want to make the team and find out what I can do. I gave up a career when I left the Navy. That should prove my confidence. But I'll never look back and regret it. If I hadn't tried to play pro ball now I'd spend the rest of my life wondering if I could have."

# The Great Quarterbacks
# Stabler ★ Kilmer
# Bradshaw ★ Staubach

★★★★★★ by Bill Gutman ★★★★★★

tempo
books

GROSSET & DUNLAP
A FILMWAYS COMPANY
Publishers • New York

Portions of this book originally appeared in the Tempo editions
*Staubach, Landry, Plunkett, Gabriel* and
*Kilmer, Hadl, Bradshaw, Phipps.*

# CONTENTS

# Stabler·Kilmer
# Bradshaw·Staubach

# ★ KEN STABLER ★

★ In the late 1960's, the University of Alabama was in its accustomed position among the top football schools in the country. The Crimson Tide and its dynamic coach, Paul "Bear" Bryant, struck fear in the hearts of most Southeastern Conference opponents whenever they took to the gridiron. Bryant was a hard taskmaster and his charges gave it their all during each and every football season.

One day during that period, Bryant gave his team a rare day off. Most of the players wanted to relax and have some fun. A small group of them went off to the nearby West Alabama Fair, figuring to mosey around, play some of the fair games, and check out the girls. As they wandered about from booth to booth, one of them noticed a target throwing game, the kind where you throw a ball at a bull's-eye. If you hit it true and hard, a mechanism is triggered and a clown, sitting in a swing, is unceremoniously dropped into a tank of cold water.

The players gathered around, eyeing up the clown, who looked at them rather suspiciously. He may have had a premonition as to what was coming. One of the boys bought a chance, got the ball, then turned to a big blond-haired youngster with an impish grin on his face.

"Here, Snake," he said, handing the ball to the youngster. "You try this."

Still grinning, the boy stepped forward, took the ball in his left hand, and without seeming to pause and aim, whipped it toward the target.

*SPLASH!*

Down went the clown into the tank, as the Alabama players roared with laughter. When the dripping clown picked himself up and returned to the swing, one of the other boys bought a chance, but instead of throwing, again handed the ball to the hard-throwing lefthander.

SPLASH!

Once again the clown flopped into the tank. He got up a third time, now hoping the boys would have had enough, taken their Kewpie doll or whatever prize they'd won, and leave. But, no, another bought a chance and once more presented the ball to the lefty, who was by now smiling broadly from ear to ear.

SPLASH!

For the third time the clown took a dip, and once again struggled back to his perch, by now trying to think of a better way to earn a living.

But the fun-loving Alabamans weren't through. They kept buying chances and giving the ball to their "hit" man. Sixteen times in all they had the southpaw flinger go after the clown, and thirteen of those times he sent the bedraggled man cascading into the cold water.

It was a lofty percentage, but it didn't really surprise the other players. For the hit man was their quarterback, Ken Stabler, who always made it a practice to hit his target, especially when throwing an oblong football on the gridiron.

In fact, on the Saturday following Ken's 13 for 16 showing at the Alabama Fair, he went out and hit on 16 of 19 real passes as Alabama defeated Mississippi, 17-7, at Jackson, Mississippi, and that's one heck of a show on enemy turf.

But that kind of thing never surprised admirers of Ken Stabler. After all, he had gone to a school that had already produced legendary quarterbacks, the likes of Bart Starr and Joe Namath, to name the two most famous ones. Yet Ken Stabler came away being called by many the best quarterback that Alabama ever had.

It seemed that he'd be a natural for professional stardom. When he was drafted by the powerful Oakland Raiders in 1968, the stage seemed set. But that's when Ken Stabler's real struggle began. Beset by personal problems and two quarterbacks ahead of him, Ken's introduction to the pros was a nightmare. On top of that, he had had knee surgery during the off-season and hadn't cared for the knee properly. He ended up spending most of his rookie year on the injured reserved list.

The following year things were worse, and in an emotional turmoil, Ken Stabler walked out on the Raiders, in essence retiring from pro football before he even got started.

The move was a big surprise to a lot of people who knew Stabler. Others figured he was just another college glory guy who couldn't cut it in the pros. It took a year for Ken to get his head straight, then he came back. After that, it was almost three more years of waiting for a chance. But when it finally came in 1973, Ken was ready.

He took over as the Raider quarterback in the fourth game of the year and went on to lead the AFC in passing with a 62.7 completion percentage, including a phenomenal 25 for 29 game against Baltimore, a game which saw him connect on 14 passes in a row. The Snake had arrived, and he's been playing at an all-pro level ever since.

But the Ken Stabler story isn't all that simple, for Ken himself is not a simple man. For instance, one sportswriter, in researching a national magazine story on Ken some years back, began collecting quotes from people who knew the Snake well. This is what the writer came up with.

"He's gotta be the coolest dude that ever set foot on a football field. Never gets upset. The guy just doesn't have a temper."

"He definitely has a temper. But he shows it very seldom . . . and never in public."

"As good a natural leader as I've ever seen. Really takes charge."

"He's not what you'd call a real 'take-charge guy.' Actually he's just 'one of the boys.' "

"He is an extremely dedicated, serious-minded athlete."

"Essentially he's a party guy. Loves nothing better than to go out and have a good time."

"Tough, very tough."

"The guy is as easygoing as mom and apple pie."

"He has an awful lot of ability and is well aware of it."

"He's modest, humble, and as unaffected by his success as anyone I've ever known."

Obviously, Ken Stabler is many things to many people. He laughs (something Ken has always liked to do) when the quotes are shown to him, for by now, Ken Stabler knows himself, even if no one else does.

"There's some truth in all those statements," he says. "I guess it's because I'm a very adaptable type of guy and relate to people in many different ways. That includes my life both on and off the field. The impression people get of me depends on the kind of relationship we've established."

Ken Stabler is a friendly, personable young man with a

quick smile and an attractive Southern drawl. In fact, Ken is a Southerner through and through, having been born in Foley, Alabama, on Christmas Day, 1945. Santa Claus couldn't have delivered a better present to the Stablers. They had a happy-go-lucky, friendly youngster, who always excelled at everything he did.

Maybe it was because things always came easy for Ken that he found plenty of time to horse around. As he grew older, he became a pretty wild kid.

"I was always in some kind of trouble when I got into my teens," he once told a writer. "Some of it was pretty bad . . . stealin', fightin', drinkin'. I guess I just liked a good time. I remember once at Alabama I bought a car and didn't have a penny in the bank and no income. Sure enough, I went out and wrecked it before I even paid for it."

Yet when Ken reached Foley High he quickly became a major star in three sports—football, basketball, and baseball. He was the quarterback on the football team, and naturally a fine lefthanded pitcher in baseball. He was also a great basketball player, averaging 29 points a game and making the all-state team two seasons in a row.

It was at Foley High that he acquired his nickname, Snake. Being an all-purpose player on the gridiron, Ken ran back punts and kickoffs, played defense, as well as quarterbacking the team. One day he dropped back to his own 30 to field a high punt. Then he took off, zigzagging up field, faking tacklers, side-stepping and slithering his way 70 yards for a touchdown. As he came to the sidelines, his excited coach ran up to him and yelled, "Boy, you ran that one back just like a snake!"

The name stuck, though by the time his career at Foley ended he was known more for his bulletlike lefthanded passes than for his running. And by this time Ken was a big guy, already at his full height of 6-3, with his weight moving over the 200-pound mark. Despite his reputation as a fun-lover, he was in demand at colleges all over the area. Yet his choice seemed very logical. Where else would Ken Stabler go than the University of Alabama?

Ken went to Alabama in the fall of 1964, playing on the freshman team the same year that Joe Namath was finishing his Alabama career as a senior. Joe Willie would be a hard act for anyone to follow, having set many Crimson Tide passing records. But when the call came, Stabler was ready.

He took over as the Bama quarterback as a sophomore in 1965, leading the team to a fine season and into the Orange Bowl, where the club unfortunately lost. But Ken was already making a reputation as an accurate passer and fine runner. He was a leader and the man the club looked to in clutch situations.

Yet despite his success on the gridiron, he was still a wild guy off the field. Coach Bryant already noted Ken's sometimes flaky, erratic behavior, and on more than one occasion was heard to say, "You're crazy, Stabler. You've gone and lost your mind!"

To many, it was inevitable that the taskmaster coach and carefree quarterback would eventually clash. Bryant was not afraid to vent his wrath on any player. In fact, he had once suspended Namath, feeling that his total control of the team was at stake. People warned Stabler to watch his step.

Fortunately, everything fell into place for the Tide the next year. Stabler was brilliant, and his supporting cast was equally good. The team won big, week after week, as Ken continued to dazzle with his dartlike, accurate passes. By the time it was over, Stabler had set a conference record with a 64.9 completion percentage and the Tide was unbeaten and ranked number one in the nation.

Both Stabler and the club showed it was no fluke by winning the Sugar Bowl game on New Year's Day and winning it by an overwhelming 34-7 count over powerful Nebraska. The Tide were National Champions, and Ken Stabler was a first-team all-American.

What happened in the following weeks was never made quite clear. The assumption is that Ken just went out and did some hard celebrating since the season was over. At any rate, the story broke within several weeks. Unable to take the Snake's antics any longer, Bear Bryant took action. He suspended his star quarterback from the squad indefinitely. When asked for the reason, Bryant would only say one word: "Non-conformity." What that meant wasn't really clear. The only question was, how long would the suspension last? Perhaps not even Ken took it seriously until one day when he got a telegram from his predecessor at Alabama, Joe Namath. The telegram contained just three words.

*He means it!*

That woke Ken up. He paid his own way into summer school to make up some credits he was lacking and made his amends with the coach. By the time the 1967 season rolled around, Ken had been reinstated and was ready to go once more.

The Crimson Tide weren't quite as powerful as they had been the year before, but they still had a formidable team. And Ken Stabler was still the leader. In an early season game against Auburn, Ken won it by racing 49 yards through the Auburn defense for a TD in a 7-3 game. He liked to run in those days.

"I led the team in rushing one year," he recalls. "We had a lot of option plays, where I could pitch out or throw or run with the ball. I always liked to run. I guess I was quicker then because I wasn't carrying quite so much weight."

Alabama finished the season with an 8-2-1 record and an invitation to play in the Cotton Bowl. It was another all-American year for Ken, and by then Bear Bryant was talking to reporters about his left-handed QB.

On one occasion the Bear said, "Ken's the most complete athlete I've ever coached. He could always run. He's a strong, determined kid. And he has that wonderful touch throwing the football."

Remember, Bryant isn't the type of guy to throw the compliments around, and with the likes of Starr and Namath for comparison, well, that only makes the coach's words even more meaningful. In fact, during Ken's great 1966 season, Bryant was heard to say, "Stabler has the best touch on a long pass I've ever seen. And that includes Joe Namath, too."

Unfortunately, Ken's career ended on a losing note. Alabama was beaten in a close 20-16 game by Texas A. & M. in the Orange Bowl. But Stabler had done his best, even though he was operating on a creaky knee by this time. Despite the prospect of knee surgery, his future seemed bright.

The only uncertainty was the sport Ken would choose. Basketball, despite Ken's ability, was out. He hadn't continued with the sport. But he had played some baseball at Alabama and was still considered a possible major league prospect. As for Ken, he had not come out publicly to proclaim one sport over the other.

When the baseball free-agent draft rolled around, Ken became a second-round choice of the National League's Houston Astros. And by the time the NFL draft approached, there were rumors that the Astros were going to offer Ken a very substantial bonus to sign, the kind of offer that a young athlete couldn't refuse. This may have scared some NFL teams away. With so many teams competing for top talent, no one wanted to waste a high pick on a guy who might opt for baseball.

And there was still another factor, one of those things composed of a combination of myth and ignorance. Ken was a left-handed quarterback, and for some reason, southpaw chuckers had never had much success in the pass-oriented National Football League. The only real lefty QB star to emerge was Frankie Albert, and he had played in bygone days, back in the 1940's. Since then, the lefties who had tried it just couldn't cut the mustard.

The reason for this isn't clear. The probable explanation is simple. There just weren't that many left-handed quarterbacks around, and even fewer who had potential NFL ability. One of the last big-name college lefties, Heisman Trophy winner Terry Baker, had been a complete bust as a pro QB. He even switched to running back before his brief career ended. So despite Ken's undisputed success at Alabama, some of the other teams just didn't want to try their luck with a lefty.

Fortunately for Ken the Oakland Raiders had the luxury to gamble. The Raiders were one of the most talented clubs in the NFL and were in solid shape at the signal-calling position. They could gamble on a lefty. Yet the Raiders, with a successful 1967 season, didn't pick until the 25th spot on the first round. In fact, the team was so good that it finished the 1967 season with a 13-1 mark and made a trip to the Super Bowl, losing to the legendary Green Bay Packers.

Even then, the Raiders passed by Ken in the first round. But when they came to pick again, Ken was still available and they took him. That made Stabler the 51st pick of the league. It was hard to believe that there were 50 college players better than Ken.

Now that he had to face reality, Ken decided that he had a better chance to make it in football, rather than baseball. The man who ran the Raiders, owner-general manager-former coach Al Davis, was very high on Stabler. Davis helped convince Ken that football and the Raiders were for him. So Ken signed, for a modest salary and bonus. It wasn't one of those huge contracts. Ken would have to prove himself on the field. But it had always been that way before, so he welcomed the challenge.

But there were some problems almost immediately. First of all, Ken had knee surgery following his season at Alabama and the knee was slow to respond. He definitely wouldn't be ready by the time training camp opened.

In addition, the Raider success in 1967 also was a triumph for quarterback Daryle Lamonica. Lamonica had been a sub at Buffalo for four seasons, and when traded to the Raiders he really opened up, passing for 3,228 yards and 30 touchdowns. He was only 27 years old then and emerged as one of the top passers in the game. How could Stabler possibly beat him out? And with the Raiders thinking Super Bowl again, it seemed as if Lamonica, barring injury, would stay at the helm. Besides, Daryle's backup was veteran George Blanda, who was used to the pressure of pitching relief. If the Raiders needed a lift, it would undoubtedly be Blanda, not Stabler, who would get the call.

The whole thing became academic in 1968, since Ken's knee continued to trouble him. Since there was no real emergency at quarterback, the club decided to put Ken on the injured reserve list for the season. So as an NFL rookie in 1968, Ken Stabler never suited up, never threw a pass, never got in a game.

Without Ken, the Raiders continued as a highly successful club. They were 12-2 for the year, losing to the New York Jets, 27-23, in the final playoff game before the Super Bowl. Though missing out on the big one, the Raiders still showed everyone they were one of the powerhouse teams in the league. Lamonica had another great year, with more than 3,000 yards and 25 more touchdowns to his credit. Stabler was just about a forgotten man when he reported to camp for the 1969 season.

It hadn't been a good off-season for Ken. He was having bad personal problems in the form of a marital breakup. Because of the stress from that he hadn't taken care of himself physically. And without continual rehabilitation, his knee was not 100 percent. He couldn't move well, and this provided another form of frustration for him. On top of this, everyone was talking about Lamonica, and how he had emerged as one of the best quarterbacks in football, a game-breaking long passer who would lead Oakland back to the Super Bowl. Ken began figuring that even if he was healthy there'd be little or no chance of playing. For the first time in his life he was really deflated. So many things seemed hopeless. So Ken Stabler reacted in a very uncharacteristic way.

He quit!

"Yes, it was very uncharacteristic of me," Stabler admitted later. "Usually I'm capable of taking everything in stride, but the frustration of everything became too much. Maybe it was a cop-out, but I was fed up with the entire situation. I didn't even tell anyone what was on my mind. One day I just busted out. I went back to Tuscaloosa [Alabama] and really raised hell."

It was a tortuous time for Ken. He had walked out on one of pro football's finest organizations. He didn't think they'd ever want him back. And as he watched the papers he saw the Raiders continue to win and Lamonica continue to heave TD passes. He was a lost soul.

"The Raiders finally got hold of me, but I was still depressed and told them I was tired of football and the whole mess. I don't think they expected me to come back."

So Ken sat out the 1969 season. Without him the Raiders were 12-1-1, once again losing in the final playoff before the Super Bowl. Lamonica had a third straight 3,000 yard season, leading the pros with 34 TD tosses. It was pretty obvious that no one around Oakland missed Ken Stabler in the least.

But the year off gave Ken plenty of time to think, to

try to get his head straight and clear up the problems in his life. By early 1970 he had reached some conclusions and found some answers.

"I had plenty of time to evaluate myself," he recalls. "I was divorced and could again look at the future. All I'd ever done was to compete and play ball. I would never have gone to college if it hadn't been for football. What the hell was I going to do now? Sell something? Hell, I couldn't sell anything. If someone told me they didn't want it I'd probably say, 'Fine, let's go get a drink.'

"I knew that I still wanted to be a ballplayer. It's the only emotion I ever had since I was old enough to play catch. Finally I realized that I better get my tail back there and go to work."

Ken wasn't even sure if the Raiders would want him. If they didn't, he'd just try elsewhere. But Al Davis still believed in his ultimate ability and was convinced that Ken deserved a second chance.

The Raiders accepted Ken back into camp with open arms. Most of the players and coaches understood his problems. Once they saw how hard he was working and how determined he was to make the team there were no hard feelings. With his mobility back, Ken quickly showed he had poise and the skills to be a pro quarterback. Now it was a matter of getting playing time. That wouldn't be easy.

For 1970 turned into the season of George Blanda. The remarkable Mr. Blanda was 43 years old that season, and had been mainly the team's placekicker the past several campaigns. But he was still a good relief QB who responded well under pressure, and whenever Lamonica faltered, Blanda came in. Several minor injuries and a growing inconsistency on Lamonica's part brought Blanda to the fore again and again. Suddenly, it seemed as if he was winning games for the Raiders week after week, either with his passing or his clutch kicking.

When the season ended the Raiders won another divisional title, only their record dropped to 8-4-2. Though Lamonica's stats were down, he still threw for 20,500 yards and 22 TD's, while Blanda came off the bench to pitch for another six scores. Ken finally got into a pro game, in fact, he got in a couple. But he only threw seven passes all year long. In essence, it was lost season number three since Ken had graduated from Alabama. But he took it in stride. At least he was on the team. Now he had to believe his chance would come.

There was a growing frustration within the Raider organization. Since reaching the Super Bowl after the 1967 season, the club had been stopped on the final plateau. This time they were beaten by Baltimore, 27-17, in the AFC title game. Some people were even beginning to say the club couldn't win with Lamonica, despite his glowing record of the past several seasons. They began to say he was a bomb-happy quarterback who threw too many long passes and panicked in the closing minutes of a tight game. A few people even began to say that Ken Stabler deserved a chance to show his stuff.

Finally, it began to look as if he might get that chance. In the fourth game of the 1971 season Lamonica was injured early and Ken came off the bench. He called a cool game and led the Raiders to a 27-16 victory, his first as a pro. Though Lamonica was ready by the next week, coach John Madden decided to stick with the youngster against Pittsburgh.

Ken was nervous in his first start and called a conservative game. He stuck to short passes and his running game. By the end of the half he had completed 11 of 15 passes. But he got just 99 yards from them and failed to put any points on the board. A nervous Madden put Lamonica in at the outset of the second half and Daryle began connecting on his long stuff. The result was a 35-10 Oakland win and a return to the bench for Ken Stabler.

Ken played sporadically for the rest of the year as the Raiders finished at 8-4-2 once again and this time failed to make the playoffs. For the year, Ken threw 48 passes, completed 24 for 268 yards and one TD. His frustration was growing.

By the outset of 1972, Coach Madden and the Raider brass were undecided about their quarterback. Lamonica was a known quantity. The new zone defenses seemed to be taking the long pass away from him, and his favorite deep receiver, Warren Wells, was no longer on the team. Stabler was still untested, but everything in his past said he was a winner. It seemed as if Ken might finally get a full shot.

It seemed even more so when he was named the starting quarterback in the opening game against the Steelers. Who knows, if Ken had had a spectacular game he might have had the job for keeps. But he didn't. In fact, it was a bad game for all the Raiders. The club was sloppy and out of tune. On several occasions receivers dropped good passes, and on several others, Ken missed his men. At the outset of the fourth quarter Lamonica was in the game. The Raiders seemed to come to life, rallied, and just missed pulling it out, losing 34-28. The result: Stabler was back on the bench. And this time he didn't like it.

For the first time since he rejoined the Raiders in 1970, Ken began thinking that he might have to make his mark somewhere else.

"All I want is a chance," Ken would say. "Any player who puts on a uniform and is satisfied being on the second team is cheating himself. It's a frustrating thing not playing when you think you should be playing. It's the hardest thing I've gone through since being in pro football."

Once again Ken was a mop-up man, getting in when the game was out of reach either way, sometimes being forced to gamble and not really play it his way. But after that first loss the club began to rally. In fact, they closed the year with six straight wins to finish at 10-3-1 and make it into the playoffs once again.

The playoff game with the Steelers that year was a memorable one. It was an epic defensive battle. By the start of the final period, two Roy Gerela field goals had given the Steelers a 6-0 lead. Lamonica was playing poorly, not moving the team at all. In a move that might have approached desperation, Coach Madden installed Ken Stabler in the game.

Ken was ready. He stayed cool and moved the team. As the time ticked away, Ken had the Raiders driving. With the ball on the Pittsburgh 30, the Snake dropped back to pass. His receivers were all covered and Ken began scrambling. He rolled right, then back to his left. Suddenly it was Alabama all over again, with Ken Stabler running down the sideline and picking up blockers.

No chance to throw now, so Ken turned on the old speed. There was the goal line, right in front of him. Then he was crossing it, a 30-yard touchdown run. Blanda's kick gave the Raiders a 7-6 lead. With time running out, it looked as if Stabler had brought the Raiders home and into the AFC title game. But the Steelers had one more chance.

Finally it came down to one play. Pittsburgh was deep in its own territory and quarterback Terry Bradshaw dropped back for a desperation pass. He threw the ball over the middle where Raider safety Jack Tatum deflected it. It seemed over.

But before the ball hit the ground, Pitt fullback Franco Harris, trailing the play, lunged for it and made a shoe-string catch. Without breaking stride, the big fullback rambled past the surprised Raiders to the end zone. It was a score, a freak score, but it gave Pittsburgh a 13-7 win, stopping the Raiders once again.

So the glory that Ken Stabler thought he had finally

earned was taken away. At least temporarily. If nothing else, Ken's clutch performance seemed to have thrust him squarely into the Raider quarterback plans for 1973. Yet he continued to talk about his frustrations in not playing.

"I hardly played at all in 1972 as far as I was concerned," he said. (He had thrown some 74 passes, completing 44 for a 59.5 completion percentage and four scores.) "It's really hard when you're not playing. Face it, we're all on big ego trips up here. Everybody wants to play, to get the recognition, to have people come up and say, 'Hey, you had a good game last week.' The money is important, of course, but it's the recognition that counts. Everybody thinks he should be playing, and it's really hard to go out there and practice your best when you know you won't be playing."

The two quarterbacks split the duties in the pre-season. Ken was looking good. His style wasn't like Lamonica's. Ken didn't throw long as often. In fact, he liked the short and medium stuff. He kept telling people he should be playing. He even would talk about his days at Alabama, perhaps because he hadn't really known the glory since.

"Bear Bryant was my greatest influence," he said. "He taught me about self-sacrifice, discipline, and doing what you're supposed to do in order to win. You depend on others, and others depend on you. I learned that you have a certain obligation to your teammates. Essentially, Bryant taught me all about playing quarterback—except how to throw.

"I take my football very seriously and I play it pretty much by the book. Unless there are some very extenuating circumstances, when I'm told to do something, I do it."

Stabler was telling the Raiders that he was willing to do anything, just to get a chance. His hopes were high. But when 1973 began, the Raiders opted for experience once more. Daryle Lamonica was back on the field directing the offense. And Ken Stabler was really chomping at the bit.

"I felt it was going to be more of the same old thing," he said. "I felt I wasn't going to get a real chance to play. I went to Al Davis early and told him I thought I wasn't his kind of quarterback and that if I wasn't going to play here I wanted to be traded someplace where I could play."

Davis had a quick answer. He told Stabler to go stand on his head.

When the "trade me" speech didn't work, Ken re-evaluated his situation.

"I looked around and thought there wouldn't be many clubs that would want to make a trade right now, so it wouldn't do me any good to keep asking to go elsewhere. But I was still determined not to go through another year like the last two. I'd pump gas first."

Everyone's frustration continued when the Raiders lost two of their first three games, and under Lamonica, the offense failed to score a single touchdown. The one highlight was a 12-7 victory over world champion Miami, which had been undefeated in 1972. The Raider victory broke the Dolphin winning streak and it gave Ken a thrill, since he held the ball for all four of George Blanda's field goals.

"Everybody was excited when we won that one," he recalls, "and I was part of the excitement since I held for George. But I wasn't real happy. I wanted to play fulltime. I wanted to be the quarterback."

Holding for Blanda's kicks helped Ken in more ways than one. He became very close to the aged veteran and on more than one occasion Blanda kept Ken from losing his cool.

"I'd say, 'George, I'm tired of this,'" related Ken, "'I wanna go someplace and play.' George would tell me to 'Hang in there and things will work out for the best.'"

But how long could Ken hang in there? Time seemed to be running out. Finally, in the third game of the year, this one against Kansas City, Madden sent Stabler in late in the game, asking him to put points on the board. The Raiders were pinned down inside their own ten yard line and all the Chiefs knew Ken had to throw. Stabler took the snap and dropped back into his end zone. He fired in the direction of running back Pete Banasak, but the ball bounced off Banasak's hands into the waiting arms of linebacker Willie Lanier. Lanier rambled into the end zone to put the game on ice. And Ken Stabler was burning. Now he had to take action.

"Two days after the game I had had it," Ken says. "I burst into Coach Madden's office and told him, 'John, I'm not going into a ballgame in that kind of situation again. I'm sorry, but you're not going to be able to count on me in the same way you have in the past. Trade me or find yourself a new back-up or something, because I won't play under conditions like that anymore.' I walked out and I had meant every word I said."

It was a bold move, but Ken had been out of Alabama since 1967. It was now 1973 and he still hadn't had a chance to be a regular pro quarterback. Perhaps it was his fault the first two years, but since then he had been ready. Ken picks up the story again.

"That same afternoon at practice I was running the St. Louis offense. They were our next opponents. I was really loose because I really didn't care anymore. I felt great and hit on everything I threw. When we got done, Madden called me back into his office and said, 'You're our quarterback. You'll be starting on Sunday.' He said that the reason was that I hadn't quit and had been passing the ball so well. But I have a hunch that the little chat we had earlier just might have had a little something to do with it, too."

Now the question was whether Ken would get a real

shot or be yanked out as soon as the offense faltered. He put it straight to Madden and got a straight answer.

"John told me that he was going to go with me, that I didn't have to worry about Daryle looking over my shoulder because I wasn't going to come out, no matter what happened."

The word was out and Ken was suddenly surrounded by reporters. One asked him if he could move the club and put points on the board. When Ken answered yes, he found that translated into headlines which read:

*STABLER: I CAN SCORE POINTS!*

Ken laughs at that one. "What was I going to say? I'm a quarterback, and if I didn't think I could get points up on the board I wouldn't be out there. But I didn't mean it to sound as if I was bragging."

The opener for Ken wasn't easy. The Raiders continued to play sloppy football. One drive was stopped when fullback Marv Hubbard fumbled at the St. Louis eleven yard line. Ken then drove the Raiders again, only to have a potential TD pass slip through tight end Bob Moore's hands in the end zone. Another drive was halted by an interception. Still another by a holding penalty.

Finally, in the last quarter, Ken guided the offense to a touchdown, halfback Charlie Smith getting the score on a two-yard plunge. But it was enough to give the Raiders a 17-10 victory, and they dominated the action by even a bigger margin than the score indicated. And true to his word, Coach Madden never made a move toward yanking Ken and inserting Daryle Lamonica.

"I know I don't show a lot of emotion out there on the field," Ken said after it was over. "But I really heaved a sigh of relief after that touchdown. I think everybody was relieved. You get in patterns sometimes and it's hard to break out of them, and there's so much pressure because every game means so much."

That game certainly meant a lot to Ken. For it showed

he could do the job under pressure and the Raiders finally decided to stay with him. He was at the helm the next week and the week after that, and he was getting better. Raider officials realized they not only had a good quarterback, but a potentially outstanding one.

Ken quickly took charge of the Oakland offense. He used the tools he had at hand. The wide receivers, Fred Biletnikoff and Mike Siani were both "moves" men, neither being a speed burner or real deep threat. So Kenny switched to a conservative short- and medium-range passing game. He felt he could move the team better that way and use more of the clock in doing so.

He was a cool operator who knew how to stay in the pocket and wait until the last split-second before throwing, even if it meant taking a solid hit from a charging lineman. And when he had to move out of there he was good at it. At 6-3, 215 pounds, he was big and strong enough to run with authority, and still quick enough to escape his pursuers.

He was also showing the fans and coaches that a left-handed quarterback could complete passes with anyone. He had a short, compact style of throwing and his passes were unerringly accurate. Someone soon said he looked as if he were throwing darts, and the phrase stuck. From then on, Stabler was a dart-thrower to most announcers, writers, and fans.

Before long, Ken made everyone aware that he was not only having a good season, but a remarkable one. First of all, he was hitting on over 60 percent of his passes, an unusually high percentage. In two separate games he threw for more than 200 yards. Then he set his 25 for 29 record against Baltimore (a mark since broken), including 14 straight completions at one point. The Raiders were winning and there was no chance of getting Stabler out of there.

It's interesting to look at the role reversal that took

place on the Oakland team. Now Daryle Lamonica was second-string. With all those great years behind him and still just 32 years old, Lamonica found the bench as hard to take as Ken had before him. He talked openly about his feelings and about the difference in the two quarterbacks.

"This has been a frustrating year for me," he said. "I'm happy that the team is winning and heading for the playoffs. That's what the game is ultimately about. But I'm a football player and I don't like not playing. I don't regard myself as a number two quarterback. As far as I'm concerned, I'm still number one."

Lamonica's words seemed all too familiar to Stabler. Just a few short months earlier he was saying the same thing. There is a deep pride within most football stars, especially those who have tasted the smell of success. It's hard for them to change. Lamonica even continued to defend his propensity to throw long passes, a tendency which earned him the nickname of "The Mad Bomber."

"Ken's style and my style are different in that I look for the big play and he likes to peck, peck, peck," said Daryle. "It's still my feeling that you have to look for the big play. You win with the big play. Even with these zone defenses the big play is there. You just have to be more patient and set it up. Eventually you'll get somebody isolated man for man."

Then Daryle talked about another, perhaps little known aspect of being number two, something that makes it harder for a number two to become number one.

"I don't get as much practice time as I did," he said. "The number one quarterback has to get most of it. So I don't really feel that I'm sharp. My timing on the exchanges isn't what it should be, so if I do get in, it limits me in the things I want to do."

Almost every NFL quarterback has experienced this kind of think sometime during his career. QBs have a fraternity all their own. Ken Stabler is very aware of the things quarterbacks must endure.

"You'll never hear me say anything bad about other quarterbacks," Ken says, "Because I know that whatever it is they're going through, either I've been through it, or chances are that I'll go through it someday. For instance, I've never been booed. I don't know how I'd react to something like that. But I really don't think I'd like it much. But if it can happen to someone as great as Johnny Unitas, then I'm sure it'll happen to me."

But none of that was about to happen in 1973. The fans of the Raiders did nothing but cheer for their new quarterback. The team was again looking like the powerhouse of years past and now everyone looked to Stabler to do the one thing Daryle Lamonica and others couldn't do: take the Raiders into the Super Bowl and win it.

Ken continued to throw darts. When the season ended he had brought the Raiders home with a 9-4-1 mark, not as good as in some previous years, but good enough to take another AFC Western Division championship.

And on the way to that title, Ken Stabler compiled some pretty fancy passing stats, good enough to be ranked as the top thrower in the AFC. He completed 163 of 260 passes for a marvelous 62.7 percent. That was good for 1,997 yards and 14 touchdowns. Just 10 of his passes were intercepted. And he did it with little more than the experience of a rookie.

"Ken's a natural quarterback," said his coach, John Madden. "He has an instinct for the game that you can't teach. He knows defenses and he has a knack for finding the open man."

It wasn't hard for Ken to find the open man in his first taste of playoff action. The Raiders were meeting rival Pittsburgh, and Stabler was magnificent. He was on target 14 times in 17 tries as the Raiders overwhelmed the Steelers, 33-14. People were beginning to feel it might finally be Oakland's year. But standing between them and the Super Bowl were the mighty Miami Dolphins, the defending champions.

The Dolphins were at the peak of their power and were devastating throughout the playoffs. Before the Raiders could get untracked, Miami exploded for two touchdowns and a 14-0 lead. That put Ken in the unenviable position of having to play catch-up football. Despite the fact that he was behind, Ken still managed to complete 15 of 23 passes, though the Miami defense toughened when it had to as the Dolphins cruised home with a 27-10 victory, their second step en route to a second consecutive Super Bowl victory.

For the Raiders, it was another bitter defeat. Losing in the AFC championship game was becoming an increasingly bad habit, and more and more people were starting to say that the team, as good as it was on both offense and defense, couldn't win the big one.

The one thing the Raiders did discover was a brilliant new quarterback, one who was young enough to continue leading them for years to come. But before the team could really rest easy with that thought, there was another shocking surprise.

It came early in the off-season. Ken announced that he had signed a multi-year, multi-million dollar contract with the Birmingham Americans of the new World Football League!

The news was a real blow. It was true that the new WFL had been "raiding" some NFL teams and had already signed some NFL stars. Larry Csonka, Jim Kiick, Paul Warfield, Calvin Hill, and Ted Kwalick were just some of the NFL superstars who had signed with the WFL. They had to remain in the NFL for their option year of 1974, then would join the new league in '75.

Some of those players had been unhappy with their present teams and the chance to grab the big money was too good to pass up. But Stabler? Ken had worked so hard to win the Raider QB job. Plus he was happy in Oakland and had not one, but two years left on his contract. He couldn't join Birmingham until 1976.

When questioned about his upcoming defection, Ken admitted that money was only part of the reason. The biggest thing was his love for the South, and the thought of returning to Alabama to play pro ball was too tempting.

"Things are a lot different down South," Ken said, "a lot easier. You can have a nice time, and life can be very simple. People just have more time for you in general."

But would Ken have time for the Raiders? Now that he signed with Birmingham, people wondered how he'd perform for Oakland. After all, he had not one, but two years to play in the NFL. Ken claimed his new pact wouldn't affect his attitude or performance with the Raiders.

"Oakland is a super team," he said, "a championship team. I've got two years to win a Super Bowl here and that's my goal, to win the title here and then go to Birmingham and win a championship in that league.

"It won't be easy. I know if I throw an interception or the club isn't moving there are people who are going to say, 'He really doesn't care because he's going to the WFL in two years.' I hope not too many people feel that way. I'm a competitor. I want to win. There's only one way I can do anything, and that's full speed.

"I don't set personal goals, like number of completions, touchdown passes, and other things like that. The only goal any player should have is to win. And the ultimate win is the Super Bowl. That's what I want. Because if I'm the quarterback of the team that wins the Super Bowl, then evidently I did something right along the way."

So Ken was trying to reaffirm his dedication to the Raiders in the remaining two years of his contract. Of course, he knew that he'd ultimately have to prove things on the field, and that's what he set out to do.

Unfortunately, Ken had a bad game in the opener, hitting on less than 40 percent of his passes, and the Raiders were beaten by Buffalo, 21-19. There was some talk, but Ken had plenty of time left. And the next week he started to go to work.

First Kansas City fell, 27-7, then powerful Pittsburgh, 17-0. This was followed by a 40-24 victory over Cleveland, a 14-10 conquest of San Diego, and a 30-27 win against Cincinnati. Victories over San Francisco, Denver, Detroit, and San Diego made it nine in a row. The Raiders were running away with their division, and Ken Stabler was playing better football than any other quarterback in the league.

Gone was the talk about the Snake not caring. He had been brilliant all year. And the Raider attack was more powerful than ever. When wide receiver Mike Siani was injured in the pre-season, speedy Cliff Branch was given a chance to play regularly. Branch was more than speedy, he was a world class sprinter who had once run the hundred in 9.1. He quickly showed he had plenty of football ability as well as speed, and he and Ken were soon hooking up on some long bombs, something that had been missing from the Oakland attack for several seasons.

"Cliff has added a new dimension to our offense," said Ken. "He's a real burner. If I can get him one-on-one with somebody, forget it. It's downtown. He's the most explosive player in football. He can fly."

Whenever someone mentioned the WFL at this point, Ken tried to ignore it. "I'm not connected with the WFL right now and can't be concerned about it. I'm still an Oakland Raider."

But there was also talk in some circles that the new league was already having financial troubles and there were questions as to whether the league would make it or not.

"I hope it works out," Ken finally said. "I am a little worried about it. I'd like to see the league make it and if there's a league in 1976, I'll be there. You know, I want to play football in the South, and I wouldn't have signed with any other team than Birmingham."

But the other Raiders and people around the league were anxious to talk about the Ken Stabler of 1974. He was having a great year.

"He's so cool under pressure," said Oakland guard Gene Upshaw. "He just stands back there regardless of the pressure, and if he gets knocked down or chased, he just stands back in there on the next play."

"Snake is the greatest natural leader I've ever seen," said tight end Bob Moore.

"Kenny reads everything so quickly," said wide receiver Fred Biletnikoff. "He knows where everyone is. He's amazing."

"He's got the guts of a giant," said coach Madden.

And the fleet Branch simply said, "Snake is a genius."

So it was all falling into place for Ken and the Raiders. They had a big lead in their division and were already looking to the playoffs, where two-time Super Bowl champ Miami was looming.

In early December, as the Raiders and Stabler were closing down on another great, 12-2 season, quarterback Ken burst into the headlines once again. This time everyone was surprised by the unexpected announcement. Through his attorney, Ken was moving to have his huge contract with the Birmingham Americans declared null and void. In effect, he was saying he wanted to remain in Oakland. It could have been a touchy situation, since the playoffs were approaching, and that was what was foremost on Ken's mind.

"I don't want to discuss it at this time," Ken told the

press. "I will say nothing to upset my teammates. I just want to prepare for the remainder of the season and the playoffs so that we can reach the Super Bowl. That has always been my objective and that of the club."

Ken's lawyer, Henry Pitts, explained further. "Ken wishes it could have worked out for him to play in Birmingham," said Mr. Pitts, "but economically it is not in his best interest."

The lawyer went on to explain that Birmingham had not met various financial commitments of the contract, and there was a question of exactly how much they could meet. So Ken decided he was better off staying in Oakland. Now it would be up to the courts to decide whether the contract had been violated or not.

Meanwhile it was almost playoff time. Ken finished the year with an impressive set of statistics. He completed 178 of 310 passes for a 57.4 percentage. His passing gained 2,469 yards and a league-leading 26 touchdowns. Only 12 of his passes were picked off. And even before the playoffs began, Ken learned he had been voted United Press International AFC Player of the Year. The awards were starting to roll in. Ken would later add the AP Player of the Year prize and also the distinction of being first-team all-pro. But now it was time for the Dolphins.

Many people branded the Oakland-Miami game the real Super Bowl struggle, claiming these first-round playoff opponents were the two best teams in the entire league. And the game proved more than anyone expected.

For more than three quarters the two clubs battled. Both quarterbacks, Stabler and Miami's Bob Griese, were brilliant, as the offenses dominated on both sides, despite two outstanding defenses. The lead changed hands several times, then changed again. Neither team could put it away. But with only minutes remaining, the Dolphins got a big score and took a 26-21 lead. It looked hopeless.

But Ken Stabler didn't quit. There were two minutes

and one second remaining when he stepped into the huddle, the ball on the Oakland 32, some 68 yards away from paydirt. Guard Gene Upshaw remembers.

"Kenny just walked into the huddle and said, 'We're going to have to go clutch this time because there's not much time left.' He was so cool, just like it was the first seconds of the game. You wouldn't have known there were just two minutes to play."

Nothing that came before counted now. The fans had already forgotten the 72-yard TD bomb to Branch that Ken had thrown just minutes earlier. He had to do it all over again.

Ken started the Raiders moving. He was throwing his short and medium stuff and connecting. He threw five passes on the drive and connected on all of them. That brought the ball down to the Miami eight yard line with just 26 seconds left. Ken took the snap and dropped back again.

Both lines collided and the Dolphin front four began charging. Ken rolled to his right, then was forced back left. Finally he spotted halfback Clarence Davis over the middle, releasing the ball just as he was hit by end Vern Den Herder. The pass floated to the goal line where Davis wrapped his arms around it for a score! Blanda's kick made it 28-26, Oakland, and that's the way it ended. The Dolphins would not win a third straight Super Bowl. The Raiders had beaten them in one of football's greatest games. After the game, Ken wanted to give the whole team credit for the victory.

"It was 'we,' not just me," he said. "Everyone on the offense did their jobs going down the field. One mistake and we could have been finished. But I never thought about not making it. When you think like that, you don't make it."

But the celebration was short-lived. The Raiders were in the AFC title game again, this time with Pittsburgh.

Some say the team just couldn't get "up" again after the great Miami win, others say the Steelers were just better that day. But, you guessed it, the club lost another big one. And it wasn't that close. The Steelers won, 24-13, eliminating the Raiders from Super Bowl contention once again. Despite the elation of the Miami win, this loss was a bitter pill for Ken and the Raiders to swallow.

"I keep reliving that game," said Ken several weeks later. "Every time I close my eyes I see it. I wake up thinking about it. I might be washing the car or taking out the garbage, or shooting pool, and all of a sudden the Pittsburgh game pops into my head.

"The worse thing is that it's such a long road back. We went through 20 games to get to that title game. Now we've got to do it all over again."

Ken knew that many people were calling the Raiders the NFL's premier "choke" team, always losing the big one.

"Sure, you think about those things," he said. "The only way to quit thinking about it is to win the big one. I don't know why we didn't win. I don't think it's anything you can put your finger on. We had everything it takes to win it all. I know I've searched and searched. I still can't figure it out.

"But it's another reason I hope I can be released from my Birmingham contract. To leave Oakland without a Super Bowl victory would be like leaving something undone."

Ken got his answer in early January. He was formally released from his WFL pact. It was fortunate, since the league played out the '75 season, then folded. So he never would have made it there in the first place. This way, he renegotiated with the Raiders and signed a new three-year pact.

The signing was the last act in making Ken the official field leader of the Raiders. He was there to stay, and when asked about leading, Ken gave his own version of what a quarterback had to do.

"The best way to lead is by example," he said. "I mean on the field. You get a guy who can throw 26 TD passes in a year and he's going to be easy to follow. You get a guy who isn't playing so good and all of a sudden he ain't that easy to follow anymore. The only way to lead is to go out there and play good.

"It's impossible to do any leading off the field. If I tried to be mister nice guy and wear a pinstripe shirt and wing-tip shoes, and go to church every Sunday and pat kids on the head . . . that don't make me a leader. You can lead off the field in high school or college, but in the pros everyone is an individual. Each person has his own ideas about how to dress, where to hang out, and his own set of moral values . . . and that's the way it should be. I certainly don't set the best example in the world off the field anyway."

Sure, Ken liked a good time off the field. But that wasn't all. He did more than his share of charity work, being especially interested in helping mentally retarded children. He recently donated $5,000 of his own money to the Special Olympics for retarded children, and always arranges to have some free tickets provided to Raider home games.

"I'm really concerned with the children," Ken says. "As athletes I feel we can do a lot of things that other people can't. We can take a more active role in helping the handicapped kids in the community."

During the off-season, Ken had some minor surgery on his knee, the one that was operated on at Alabama. "It's just kind of an oil and grease job," he joked, "and I'm hoping it gives me a little more mobility."

Ken was ready for the 1975 season. And the Raiders were ready for the long road back. Unfortunately, the script was all too familiar. The team was again a powerhouse, and easily booted home atop its division with an 11-3 mark. Ken had another good year with a 58.4 completion percentage and 2,296 yards. For some reason he threw more intercepts, 24, and just 16 TDs, but the club was never really pressed in the regular season.

Then came the playoffs and the same old story. First there was a brilliant win, a great game, 31-28 against Cincinnati, very similar to the Miami game of the year before. But once again the club couldn't get through the AFC title game. This time Pittsburgh beat them by a 16-10 count, as the Steelers marched on toward their second straight Super Bowl win. It marked the sixth time since 1967 that the Raiders had lost the conference title game, the game a step away from the Super Bowl.

Once again Ken and his teammates had to live with the choke label. And once again they had to prepare for the long road back. On paper, the Raiders had been pro football's most successful regular season team for more than a decade. Their record had been outstanding. But they hadn't won the big one. And that had been a monkey on all their backs.

As for Ken, he was ready for a long run. "How long a player does something well is the only way to judge him, and the only way he can prove himself. I've got a long way to go yet, and some day we're all gonna win the whole thing."

So in 1976 the Raiders again set out to win the whole thing. As many people had said, there were two seasons for the Raiders. First there was the regular season, in which they breezed to the divisional title as if it were automatic. Then came the playoffs in which they always managed to blow the big game.

They seemed to be following the same pattern in '76. They won game after game, and had all but wrapped up the division by midseason. Once again it was Stabler and his receivers, a good running attack, and a powerful defense.

Ken seemed sharper than ever. The old dart-thrower still had that magic touch. Give him a second and he'll pass you to death, that's the way many football people put it. He did plenty of that, but still passed only when he had to. He was a patient, controlled field leader.

It was a super year for Ken and the Raiders. The team had a 13-1 mark, the best in football. But that was old hat. What they had to do was win the Super Bowl. Anything less would mean the same old criticisms.

As for Ken, he had thrown 291 times, completed 194 for a sensational 66.7 percent. That was the best percentage of any NFL quarterback since Sammy Baugh's record 70.3 percent in 1945. In addition, Ken passed for 2,737 yards, had a league leading 27 TD passes, and was intercepted just 17 times. Statistically, he was the leading passer in the entire NFL.

The playoffs were another story. Season stuff was forgotten. In fact, the Raiders almost failed to get past the first round. They had to face the upstart New England Patriots, the team that had handed them their only loss during the regular campaign.

It was a hard-fought game that saw the lead change hands several times, but in the closing minutes the Patriots led, 21-17. The Raiders needed a TD or it was over. Ken coolly began driving his team. With less than a minute to go he had them on the one. Finally he took it himself and dove over the left side of the line for the winning score. Ken had saved his club from another humiliating defeat. The Raiders won it, 24-21, and would now meet Pittsburgh for the AFC crown. The Steelers had eliminated the Raiders the two previous years.

This time the Raiders got a break. Pittsburgh was missing both its 1,000-yard runners, Franco Harris and Rocky Bleier, who'd been hurt the week before. This crippled the Pittsburgh offense and put too much strain on the defense.

Ken called a very smart, conservative game. He threw only when he had to, and let his runners and his defense set things up. He had his club ahead, 17-7, at the half, then fired his second TD pass in the third period to make it 24-7. That's the way it ended, with the Raiders finally taking the AFC crown. Ken was just 10 for 16 for 88 yards. But that's the way he wanted it.

"We shut a lot of mouths today," said a happy Stabler. "There were all those people who said we'd fold up in the championships. They said we were a dirty team and we were going to lay down in a big game. We had to alibi for ourselves all year and now we went out and got it done."

There was more to it than the Pitt injuries. Ken and his mates had put 24 points on the board against a defense that had registered five straight shutouts during the regular season. Now the Raiders were at the summit. The last barrier was the Minnesota Vikings, the NFC champs. But the Vikes also had something to prove. They had come up losers in three previous Super Bowl games. So both clubs wanted it badly.

As usual, there was a great deal of hoopla preceding the game, which was played before more than 100,000 fans in the Rose Bowl at Pasadena, California. The Vikes were still formidable. They had wily Fran Tarkenton at QB, a great all-around back in Chuck Foreman, and an explosive rookie receiver in Sammy White. Plus the great, tough aging, defense. Most figured the game a tossup.

But the Raiders planned carefully. Ken started out slowly. He used his runners and his great offensive line, hoping to wear down the older Vikes. Soon the formula was working. Clarence Davis was especially effective, reeling off several big gains.

The game was a standoff in the first period. But to many, it seemed like a matter of time. Sure enough, in the second period the Raiders began moving. First Errol Mann booted a 24-yard field goal. Minutes later Ken had his team moving again. He capped this one with a little play-action TD pass to tight end Dave Casper from the one. It was now 10-0.

Before the half, Ken moved the club again. This time veteran halfback Pete Banazak scored from the one. The extra point was missed, but at halftime it was 16-0. Still, the Raiders couldn't afford to let down. And they didn't.

Ken was loose now. He completed six straight passes before halftime. As team general manager Al Davis explained, "Kenny was mad at himself early in the game when he kept running on third down. We had made a vow not to tighten up and I guess Kenny figured it was time to unglue a little."

Stabler also showed his leadership qualities in the first half. Coach John Madden was upset when the Raiders drove the length of the field two times early in the game and got just one field goal out of it.

"Kenny grabbed my arm," said Madden, "and told me, 'Don't worry, there's a lot more where that came from. We're gonna get you a lot of points today.' "

Mann kicked a 40-yarder early in the third period, but then Minnesota came back to score on a Tarkenton to White pass. It was 19-7, and still a game. Then Ken took charge once more. He drove his club downfield with some clutch passes, then let Banazak go over from the two. Minutes later veteran cornerback Willie Brown put the game on ice by intercepting a Tarkenton pass in the flat and scampering 76 yards for the score. That broke the Vikings' backs. A meaningless TD came in the closing minutes. The Raiders had won, 32-14. They were champions of the world.

Finally!

"I told you we were gonna win this thing one of these

years," a happy Stabler said. "Can't say I'm sorry it happened now."

Wide receiver Fred Biletnikoff was the game's MVP for some marvelous catches of Stabler passes. Ken was conservative. As usual, he did what he had to do, completing 12 of 19 for 163 yards. He had called and played a brilliant game.

The plaudits for Ken didn't end with the Super Bowl. A few weeks later he learned he was the winner of the S. Rae Hickok Award as the Professional Athlete of the Year. In winning the award, Ken beat out a couple of outstanding performers, Cincinnati Reds MVP second baseman, Joe Morgan, and tennis superstar Chris Evert.

Perhaps a prize like the Hickok Award was long overdue. Those who have known Ken Stabler know he is a winner. He always has been. Now he's being called the greatest left-handed quarterback ever, and before he's through some of those people might just drop the "left-handed" qualification. For Ken "Snake" Stabler is that good.

WITH KILMER

quarterbacks."

# ★ BILLY KILMER ★

★ Bill Kilmer has always had a reputation as a certain
kind of guy. His guts and determination have been
admired and respected for a long time, even before he
attained his current star status with the Washington Redskins.

One of the greatest of all professional quarterbacks,
Bart Starr, used to tell a story on the banquet circuit
whenever someone asked him how he became the Packer
quarterback. The tale really had no connection with Kilmer, that is, until a former pro football coach heard it one
night. It went something like this:

"When Coach Lombardi came to Green Bay the first
thing he did was build a large brick wall at the end of the
field. Then he told all the players to run toward it full tilt.
The ones who banged into it and fell backwards became
defensive lineman. Those who cracked into it and fell on
their stomachs became offensive linemen. The ones who
ran through it were the fullbacks, and the ones who ran

36

up to the wall, stopped, then walked around it became quarterbacks."

After hearing this story one night, the former coach grinned and remarked, "Lombardi would have been thoroughly confused if he sent Billy Kilmer at that wall. Billy would run into it, run through it, jump over it, or walk around it . . . anything that it took to win. Lombardi wouldn't have known where to play him."

Vince Lombardi never coached Billy Kilmer. If he had, however, he would have known exactly where to play him. For one way or another, Billy Kilmer is a quarterback. He may defy convention; he may not have the natural physical attributes; he may do things his own way—but Kilmer is all quarterback.

Washington Redskin right end, Jerry Smith, no little guy himself, once looked at a bruised and battered Kilmer coming into the locker room after a game and said, "If it was three o'clock in the morning and I had to go down a dark alley, I'd want him with me."

That kind of respect doesn't come easy, but William Orland Kilmer earned it, and he didn't do it the easy way. After all, it's not many quarterbacks who are told:

They may not live.

They may lose a leg.

They will never play football again.

And it isn't every quarterback who can sit on a professional bench for the better part of three seasons seeing less action than the water boy, then bounce back with a display of skills people never knew existed. But Billy Kilmer did it.

On December 24, 1972, an overflow crowd gathered in Washington's Robert F. Kennedy Stadium to watch their beloved Redskins do battle with the Green Bay Packers in the first round of the National Conference playoffs.

The hometown fans hooted and cheered as each Redskin starter was introduced and trotted onto the field. But they saved the longest and loudest cheers for number 17, their quarterback, a 33-year-old veteran named Billy Kilmer.

Fans watching Kilmer jog confidently onto the field and begin exhorting his teammates with shouts and smacks on the back wouldn't have known it was the same man who, exactly 10 years earlier, lay flat on his back in a San Francisco hospital fighting for his life, his leg, and his professional career. Lombardi's brick wall would have looked awfully big to him then.

Kilmer had come to the Skins in 1971, in the first of many trades engineered by new head coach George Allen. After struggling at San Francisco and taking his lumps with expansionist New Orleans, Kilmer should have been happy going to the rebuilding Redskins. But he wasn't, and that was because the Washington team had a quarterback named Sonny Jurgensen, widely regarded as one of the best passers ever. The thought of once again being a backup didn't appeal to this competitive fireball from Topeka, Kansas.

But Allen knew what he wanted. When someone questioned the trade, the coach snapped, "Kilmer is a fighter. He never quits. He's done a tremendous job at New Orleans. He's the kind of competitor and leader I want around here. No matter where I was coaching I'd want him. He'll be ready whenever we need him."

The need came. An injury to Jurgensen in the exhibition season made Kilmer number one for the entire 1971 season. And what did he do? He led the Washington Redskins to their best record in 29 years and into the NFL playoffs. Like the man said, when they needed him, Billy Kilmer was ready.

There was a time when William Orland Kilmer wasn't ready. It was by no fault of his, however. Bad luck seemed to dog the gritty quarterback from the beginning of his career.

Not from the beginning of his life, though. That was a happy time. Billy was born in Topeka on September 5, 1939. When he was just a youngster his parents moved to California where his father, Orland Kilmer, opened a dry cleaning business. Mr. Kilmer was away from home some 10 to 12 hours a day, and when young Bill saw his first football game it was with his grandfather at the Los Angeles Coliseum.

"I guess I was about five then," Bill recalls. "I know that my feet wouldn't even reach the floor when I sat in the chair. Anyway, my grandfather took me to the game and I can remember sitting in the crowded stands and thinking even then that I wanted to be just like those football players on the field. It just looked so great to be playing in front of so many people. I told my grandfather that I wanted to be a football player when I grew up. I don't know if he believed me, but we were always great pals and he took me to a game almost every week."

Grandpa Kilmer wasn't the only member of the family to encourage young Bill in athletics. His mother had once pitched on a ladies softball team that won the Women's World Series at Soldier Field in Chicago, and she still got a kick out of pitching the ball to her son in the backyard of their home. So that took care of football and baseball.

Orland Kilmer handled the basketball end of it. He put up a board and hoop in the yard and Billy used to shoot at it for hours on end.

"It was a great way to relieve my frustrations," said Billy. "Whenever I wanted to think about something or make some plans, I'd go out and shoot baskets. That's when I got my ideas."

And that wasn't all. Mr. Kilmer had been Missouri Valley swimming champion and once had an opportunity to try out for the Olympic team. As a result, swimming came easily to Bill and he could hold his own in the water with anyone.

When he got to junior high school he began putting his all-around athletic skills to work and he quickly found out something about himself.

"I loved competition," Bill recalls, "right from the first. It was the challenge to win. I always wanted to be the very best at everything I did."

When Billy arrived at Azusa High School, he was a multi-sport star, a performer for all seasons who electrified the Azusa fans with his exploits on the playing fields. At first, the six-foot, 190-pound Kilmer preferred basketball. He liked the constant movement and hectic non-stop action of the court game. He was a standout at guard, ball-handling, driving, and jump-shooting with the best of them. He led the Azusa team to a near-perfect record for three seasons. The team lost just one league game in that time and Kilmer became Southern California scoring champion, pumping nearly 2,000 points through the hoop in three seasons.

But he didn't neglect the other sports. He may not have liked baseball as much, but he played the game with consummate skill. In fact, by the time he was a senior the scouts were coming around in droves and the word on Kilmer was out. There was talk of a $50,000 bonus with the Pirates, and Billy liked the sound of that.

"I was all set to sign and leave for training camp," he revealed, "but my mother intervened. She was determined that I go to college and my father agreed. Then I thought it out and decided it was the right thing.

"Besides, by then I was really in love with football. That's why I chose UCLA. They still played the single wing formation and I wanted a chance to be a tailback. I wanted to be a triple-threat man—running, passing, and kicking. There weren't too many of those guys left anymore."

So, after a year at Citrus Junior College, Billy went to UCLA with the prime objective of playing tailback. But what is a tailback? You don't really hear the term much anymore.

That's because the single wing as an offensive formation is almost completely gone today. All schools use the standard "T," the pro set, the wishbone-T, or some other variation. But in each of these cases, the play is started by the quarterback taking a direct snap from the center.

With the single wing, the quarterback was merely a blocking back, standing to the right or left of center and calling signals. He rarely touched the ball on offense. The focal point of the attack was the tailback, who stood about five yards behind the center and took a direct snap. From there, the tailback would either run, throw, or kick when necessary. Occasionally, he'd hand the ball to his fullback, who stood in the backfield with him. But more than 90 percent of the time, the tailback started the play.

When Kilmer arrived at UCLA, there were still a handful of college teams using the single wing. The UClans were among them, and there Bill could realize his long-standing dream of playing tailback. Coach George Dickerson knew the multi-talented halfback from Azusa could do it all, and immediately installed him as a tailback candidate during his sophomore year of 1958.

By the end of the practice season, Bill had won the starting tailback job and opened the season against the University of Pittsburgh. It looked as if his dream was about to come true. On the first series of downs, Bill began marching the Bruins downfield. With the ball on the 40, he took a direct snap, dropped back another two or three yards, then heaved a long pass to his flanker back. The receiver gathered it in at the goal line and went over for a score.

Billy came to the sidelines, the cheers of the crowd ringing like music in his ears. He was proud and happy, and thought back to the days when his grandfather used to take him to the games. His grandfather and the rest of his family were in the stands that day and it made Billy even happier.

The UClans eventually lost that one, 27-6, but Kilmer had shown enough to win the regular tailback job. The rest of the team was young and inexperienced, but Billy was happy to be in there. He had a fine second game, helping defeat Illinois, 18-14, and with a win under his belt, looked forward to meeting another single win team, Oregon State, the next week.

Then, early in the game, it happened. There was a pileup on a running play and Bill got up holding his right hand. Someone had stepped on it and he left the game. X-rays showed a broken bone and he was out. Terribly disappointed, the combative Kilmer had to sit the bench until the final game. Against USC he saw limited action, played well, and was instrumental in helping his team to a 15-15 deadlock.

Bill was happy to be back, but he was also thinking of the next season and a chance to redeem himself for what he considered a lost year. There were those who agreed with him; a local paper said, "Nothing is going to stop Billy Kilmer next year."

With a new coach in Bill Barnes and a more experienced team, the Bruins looked to a big year. Barnes was counting on Kilmer as his starting tailback. Then fate took a hand once again.

Umpiring an intramural baseball game, Bill was struck on his ankle by a foul ball. The ankle wasn't broken, but bruised severely enough to shelve him once again. This time he couldn't run, and by the time the season was almost over, he was out of shape and overweight. He struggled to get ready, and with the ankle still tender, managed to get into the last five games.

He saw some action against Stanford and North Carolina State, then came back against unbeaten USC. Playing in sneakers because his ankle was too sore for football cleats, the gutty Kilmer hobbled through a few running plays. But mostly he passed—and he was on target. When the day ended, the Bruins were 10-3 winners, and Kilmer shared the glory with the UCLA defense, which had bottled up the Trojan attack most of the afternoon.

Bill did the same thing the following two weeks, helping to defeat Utah 21-6, then participating in a losing effort against Syracuse, 36-8. But the club had improved and managed a 5-4-1 record with everyone looking forward to the 1960 season. One writer, however, voiced cautious optimism, something everyone felt.

"For two seasons now," he wrote, "the Bruins have had a potentially outstanding tailback in young Bill Kilmer. When he's right, the experts say he's at least the equal of Paul Cameron, Primo Villanueva, Sam Brown, and Ronnie Knox, the top tailbacks since the Bruins began using the single wing a dozen years ago.

"But Kilmer has never had a chance to really show his stuff. The injury jinx has hit this youngster from Azusa, and hit him hard. A broken hand and severely bruised ankle have cost him the better part of two seasons. Now, as a senior, he has one last chance to show that he rates with the best. Let's hope he stays healthy . . . for everyone's sake."

He stayed healthy. It took a few games for him to get the feel of being a fulltime tailback, and the defense had to mature, too, but the Bruins soon showed signs of being one of the best teams in the country, with Kilmer the spiritual and physical leader.

UCLA opened with a 8-7 win over Pittsburgh, then tied Purdue at 27-all. A 10-8 loss to Washington followed, so the team was 1-1-1 after three games. But Kilmer was already making his mark. He fired three TD passes in the deadlock with Purdue, and according to most observers, outplayed Washington QB Bob Schloredt even though the Bruins lost.

After a 26-8 victory over Stanford, the Bruins edged North Carolina State, 7-0, as Billy outplayed State's Roman Gabriel, considered by many as the best T-quarterback in the country. Two big victories followed that, a 28-0 win over California, and a 22-0 whitewash of the Air Force Academy. And suddenly Kilmer was attracting national attention.

A loss to arch-rival USC followed, but Kilmer and the Bruins then closed out the year with wins over Utah and Duke. The team was 7-2-1 for the season and Kilmer had taken the total offense title.

Playing in all 10 Bruin games, Billy had carried the ball 163 times for 803 yards, averaging nearly five yards a carry. In addition, he completed 64 of 129 passes for 1,086 yards and eight touchdowns. His total was 1,889 yards, and he took the total offense crown by more than 150 yards. He completed his dream of being a triple-threat star by punting for a 42.3 yard average on 35 kicks, and that was good for fifth best in the entire country.

And he got more recognition than that. Coach Barnes called him the best tailback UCLA ever had. He was named to the Football Writers' Association and *Sporting News* All-America teams. On four occasions he was Southern California Player of the Week, and five times he was named Big Five Back of the Week. But it wasn't only on the coast. He was a two-time Associated Press National Back of the Week and twice a member of the UPI Backfield of the Week. It was quite a year, and the end of an era as well. Kilmer was the last great single wing tailback at UCLA. Soon after he left the UClans switched to the straight-T formation, as most colleges were changing their style of play.

What to do now? After all, the pros didn't play the single wing. It was the straight T all the way in the NFL. There was a time when Bill planned to go into the dry cleaning business with his father, but now football was in his blood. He had to give it a try. He was married by then, and had an infant daughter. He worried about his wife and child, but since he had the family business to fall back upon, nothing would be lost if football didn't work out.

The main problem was finding a position. He knew he could run the ball and he knew he could throw. But could he do either well enough to play halfback or quarterback in the pros? Many of the scouting reports read: Too slow to be a halfback; not a strong enough arm to be a quarterback. It looked like a dead end.

There were other T-quarterbacks that year, men like Fran Tarkenton and Norman Snead, and they were grabbed right away by the pros. Kilmer figured he'd have to wait. But then he heard the news. The San Francisco 49ers, a better-than-average club, picked him as their first draft choice.

Billy couldn't believe it. He knew that the 49ers had two fine quarterbacks in veteran Y. A. Tittle and young John Brodie. They also seemed set at halfback. He wondered just what they had planned for him.

It didn't take him long to find out. San Francisco coach Red Hickey called on Billy and explained what he had in mind. Hickey thought football was ready for a change. He planned to open the 1961 season with a new offensive formation. It was tabbed the "Shotgun," and would feature the quarterback taking a direct snap from center.

"You mean it's similar to the single wing?" an astonished Billy asked.

"Similar," said Hickey, "in that I'll need a quarterback who can run as well as pass."

"I'm your man," said Billy. And suddenly he had a new lease on life.

The shotgun wasn't a new formation. It was similar to the old double-wing, giving the offensive team an extra wide receiver. The immortal Glenn "Pop" Warner had used it at Stanford right after World War I, and several other colleges had used it on occasion. It was known as a potent passing formation, the theory being that the passer didn't have to turn his back on the field as the T-quarterback often does while retreating. The shotgun passer could watch his receivers throughout the entire pattern.

Of course, he didn't have as many options on running plays. That's why the shotgun triggerman (you couldn't really call him a quarterback) had to be able to lug leather himself. Put those prerequisites into the 1960 collegiate hopper and the answer came out K-I-L-M-E-R.

Billy was excited about beginning his professional career. But he had a stop to make first. Because of his all-around ability he was chosen to play in the annual College All-Star Game in Chicago, with the top collegians going against the world champion Philadelphia Eagles. At practice, Kilmer so impressed Coach Otto Graham that he installed Billy behind Norman Snead at the quarterback position, the T-quarterback position.

Philadelphia quickly took a lead, pushing around the inexperienced collegians without much trouble. It soon became evident that Snead couldn't move the All-Stars. Graham knew he had to shake up his team so he replaced the classic passer with the street fighter. Billy Kilmer went into the game.

Suddenly the stars seemed to come to life. With Kilmer handing the ball off, carrying it himself, and throwing, they began to move. Three times they drove upfield. The first two times the Eagle defense stiffened and held. The third time they couldn't stop Kilmer. He passed for first downs on three consecutive plays as the huge crowd roared. The Stars jumped to the line breathing fire. Kilmer barked signals, took the snap, and ran straight up the middle through the heart of the Philly defense, picking up 13 yards and another first down.

Like most great players, Kilmer is an opportunist. He knew the Eagles were down and he wanted to strike fast. He took the snap and dropped straight back. Playing the unfamiliar T didn't seem to bother him at all. He looked downfield and rifled a pass to Glynn Gregory in the end zone. Touchdown! Kilmer had thrown for a 17-yard score and the Stars were on the board.

His leadership continued throughout the rest of the game, and he drove his team to another late score. The final was 28-14 in favor of the Eagles, but Kilmer was the talk of the town. He was voted the Most Valuable All-Star Performer, something very few people would have bet on before the game began. But Billy was never one to rest on his laurels. After the game he headed right for the 49er camp, ready to start all over again.

When he got there he found that Coach Hickey was indeed working hard at the new shotgun formation. He had already made one move, deciding that veteran Tittle was too old and slow to trigger the shotgun, so he traded the old quarterback to the New York Giants. The other triggermen were Brodie, essentially a passer, and a rookie named Bobby Waters, whose forte was running the ball. Kilmer, it seemed, offered the best pass-run combination of the three.

"Since I was a single-wing tailback in college," Bill said, "this is the only possible formation that I could step into without a long period of training."

Before long, the roles of the three rotating quarterbacks became obvious. Brodie was a professional thrower all right, by far the best pure passer in the group. But he wasn't a runner of any sort. He could scamper for shelter when pursued, but couldn't do much on designed running plays. Waters, on the other hand, was quite a fine runner who might have had a shot at a halfback job. But his passing left something to be desired and it was a risk any time he threw the football.

San Francisco opened the season with a flourish as the shotgun put points on the scoreboard in bunches. And early in the season it became obvious that Kilmer was more or less the regular. Brodie came in on some passing situations, Waters when a fresh runner was needed. Kilmer himself ran much more often than he passed, but the threat of the pass was present on every play and that made him more effective.

The team was in the running during the early part of the year, but after the halfway point, some of the other clubs began to catch up with the shotgun. Most observers figured the newness of the formation accounted for its effectiveness in the early going.

"What did you expect?" wrote one newsman. "Most teams work at defensing the T. That's what they see, week after week. Suddenly, along comes the shotgun and takes them by surprise. But give them a few weeks to study it, learn what makes it tick, and they'll be ready, even the teams that haven't seen it before. That's what makes these guys pros."

But while there was now some doubt about the ultimate success of the formation, there was no doubt about Bill Kilmer's ability to run it. Just past the mid-season mark, league statistics showed that Billy was number six in the league rushing race.

"Pro football hasn't been easy for me," said the flashy rookie. "I've learned more here already than I did in my entire career before this. But with Coach Hickey calling the plays, I can concentrate strictly on execution and I think that's helped."

The last few weeks of the season were tough ones. The offense wasn't moving nearly as well as it had earlier and many were beginning to think the shotgun had run its course. The team finished with a mediocre 7-6-1 record, winding up fifth in the Western Conference of the NFL.

What had been a season of great expectations turned into a disappointment.

Statistically, Billy had an outstanding year. He had carried the ball 96 times, gaining 509 yards on an average of 5.3 yards per carry. And he was the bread-and-butter man around the goal line, scoring 10 touchdowns, including a record four in one game against the Vikings.

In the passing department, he really didn't have the chance to prove much, throwing just 34 times and completing 19 for 286 yards. Some quarterbacks do as much in a single game.

Tight end Mike Ditka of the Chicago Bears was the Rookie of the Year that season, and Bill couldn't even claim to be the best rookie quarterback. Fran Tarkenton, the freshman signal-caller of the Vikings, passed for almost 2,000 yards, and 18 touchdowns, and scrambled for 308 on the ground. When they met head to head, Kilmer helped San Francisco produce two victories, 38-24, and 38-28.

Yet Billy must have wondered what the future held. He was somewhat in limbo and wanted a chance to prove himself again. He'd have to, especially if the shotgun was abandoned.

It wasn't. Hickey wanted to give it one more try in 1962, and Billy again figured large in his plans. The young tailgunner went into the new year full of optimism, but before long he realized that it was just more of the same. In fact, it was worse. The team wasn't putting nearly as many points on the board, and it was giving up more. They weren't winning, and it was becoming obvious that the shotgun was slowly grinding to a halt.

Billy was the same kind of player in 1962. He ran much more often than he passed, and ran effectively. On the rare occasions that he did throw, his passes were wobbly, but accurate.

By the time the club had completed its first 12 games,

Bill's stats were comparable to those of his rookie season. He had rushed 93 times for 478 yards and a 5.1 average, scoring five touchdowns along the way. Passing, he was just eight of 13 for 191 yards, but that was good for another score. Although there were still two games left, it was apparent that the 49ers were not going to play .500 ball. (They finished at 6-8.)

Billy Kilmer didn't play in those final two games. In fact, for a long while it looked as if he had played his last football game ever. Bill didn't know it when he finished practice the afternoon of December 5, 1962, but he was about to embark on the biggest battle of his young life.

He left camp and began driving to the city on the Bayshore Freeway. Bill was a tired man. The team had a couple of days off before the practice and he had been on a quick hunting trip. He was drowsy as he whipped the auto along the freeway at a fast clip. It's not clear just what happened next. A car might have veered into his path, or he might have fallen asleep, but in a flash, Kilmer's car was off the road and careening down a steep embankment.

The car rolled some 435 feet through a field and into a deep ditch. In the car lay an unconscious Bill Kilmer, with a right leg badly fractured above the ankle, a severely slashed chin, and a deep gash over his right eye. He was also suffering from concussion and shock.

When rescue workers arrived, they had to use a crowbar and torch to get Kilmer out of the car. In that time muddy water from the ditch had seeped into the auto and was already causing infection in the leg. It was a nightmare.

"I'm sure I fell asleep at the wheel," Billy recalled later. "The car went off the road and began plunging into the ditch. I remember waking up as I went off. I knew if I let go of the wheel I'd be thrown out, so I held on. I figured if I went flying out anything could happen. Anyway, my right leg got caught under the brake pedal. I could feel it snap, and I could see the bone coming through."

When the doctors first examined him they weren't sure whether they could save the leg. They set the bones, and there was no real ligament damage. But the muddy water had started an infection. If it couldn't be controlled, the situation would be crucial.

Billy lay in the hospital bed for the next few days thinking about just one thing. Then he started asking questions. First he asked about the leg. They told him they could save it unless there were more complications. Then he asked about walking. They told him he'd probably never walk normally again. Finally, he asked the big one. He wanted to know if he'd ever play football again. The doctors said there was no chance.

"We'll see about that," Billy Kilmer said to himself.

The hospital stay extended to three months as the leg slowly healed and the danger of more infection ebbed. Billy just lay there all those days and not a minute passed in which he didn't think about football, about how much he wanted to play again.

"My dad came in one day and asked me what I planned to do with myself now," he recalls. "I knew, but I didn't tell him. He suggested I come into the dry cleaning business since I always said I would someday. I agreed to work with him, but I was already making plans to rehabilitate the leg."

Billy began hobbling around his father's store. Within three weeks he was doubly convinced that he had to play ball again. But he faced another operation on the leg the following June, this one to remove some floating bone chips that had accumulated. Then the doctor's work would be done. The rest was up to Bill.

He knew there was no chance to play in 1963, and he wasn't even listed on the 49er roster. The team slipped all the way to the bottom of the loop that year as Red

Hickey and the shotgun offense were both booted out the door. But Bill couldn't think about that now. His first job was to get himself back into playing shape. He'd worry about a position later.

"I had to look at it that way," he explained. "My life was athletics and I figured I was too young to give it all up. I tend to get a little stubborn, especially about things I really want . . . and this was something I really wanted. Nobody ever came out and said I *couldn't* play football any more. They just said they didn't think I would. Well, I had to find out for myself whether I could or I couldn't."

Bill worked out during 1963 and the early part of '64, pushing himself continually and slowly, ever so slowly, regaining his mobility in the ankle. He knew he might not have as much speed as he once had, but he was prepared to use whatever was left.

Then in July of 1964 it became official. Billy was rejoining the squad and would be a full playing member when training camp opened the following week. The 49ers had a new coach by then, Jack Christiansen, who promptly returned the team to the more traditional T formation. John Brodie would be the quarterback, and a strong-armed youngster from Miami, George Mira, was slated to be the backup. That left Kilmer somewhere between third string and a halfback job.

As soon as camp opened, Christiansen made it known that Billy would be used as a running back only. Kilmer didn't complain. Making the team was his first goal.

In early August the team had its first all-out scrimmage at Kezar Stadium. When Billy entered the game, the fans who had come out to watch gave him a rousing reception. Buoyed by their cheers, the former shotgun triggerman ran well and apparently without pain in his ankle. It was hard to believe. When the scrimmage ended he was the leading runner of the day with 37 yards on seven carries.

And on one play he took a hand-off, faked an end sweep, and suddenly whipped a 13-yard TD pass to Monty Stickles. Kilmer could still hurt an opponent in more ways than one.

But the music just wasn't there. It was a matter of timing, a new position, and some faster, stronger backs ahead of him. Christiansen used him sparingly all season, though there were those who felt his leadership ability and inspirational play could have helped the team, especially since a 4-10 season kept the 49ers mired in the basement.

As it was, Billy carried just 36 times for 113 yards. As an option passer he was eight of 14 for 92 yards and a score. But it wasn't much of a season. And to add even more confusion to the situation, Christiansen approached him when it was all over and said he wanted him back as a quarterback in '65.

Billy jumped at the news. In his heart, this was what he wanted to do. But he realized it wouldn't be easy. Christiansen treated him like any other player and Bill knew he had to make the team on his own. He survived the final cut, but saw little action in the exhibition games. In the final pre-season game against the Rams he got in long enough to throw three passes. They were the last three he'd throw all year. Brodie and Mira were still ahead of him, and, to make matters worse, he reinjured the bad ankle. He didn't get in for one play.

By now, even a positive thinker like Bill was becoming discouraged. Going into the 1966 season he was 27 years old and felt that his career hadn't even begun. The years of shotgun seemed like a dream. Now he was a third-string quarterback and it seemed as if he'd always been one. But he wouldn't quit, and when 1966 rolled around he was right back in there plugging.

The 49ers were a .500 team in '66, but Christiansen hoped to get them back in contention and he stuck with

Brodie most of the way. If desire counted, Billy would have been in there every play.

By the time the final game rolled around, Bill Kilmer had seen a total of ten minutes and seven seconds playing time, appearing in just three ballgames. With the club going nowhere, some of the local sportswriters were getting restless.

One noted how Kilmer never left Christiansen's side during the ballgames, as he tried to get as close to the action as he could. The writer noted that "his (Kilmer's) burning desire to play, coupled with Christiansen's refusal to let him do so, except infrequently, made for a pathetic frustration."

But Billy Kilmer is the kind of guy people believe in. That became evident early in 1967. The National Football League was expanding once more and a new franchise was being added in New Orleans. As with all expansion teams the Saints, as they were called, wanted some solid veteran players around whom to build a respectable club.

Looking over the crop of back-up and veteran quarterbacks, the Saints quickly made their first choice. They picked Billy Kilmer.

There was no doubt about Bill's reaction. He was happy that he'd finally have a chance to play ball, even though the Saints were an expansion club, a place where the quarterback is often not much more than a glorified punching bag. But he was confident and defiant.

"I'm not afraid of being hit, so you won't find me looking for the ends, tackles, and linebackers when I drop back to pass. I'll be looking for my receivers. If you start worrying about the guys who are coming after you, then you might as well just run away and hide.

"This is the chance I've been waiting for. The 49ers used me in one exhibition game a year. They had no room for me and I wanted to go someplace where I could play. That's all I ever wanted, a fair opportunity."

By the time the exhibition season started, the Saints had picked up another quarterback, Gary Cuozzo, who had been an impressive back-up to John Unitas at Baltimore. Cuozzo was a standard dropback passer with a good arm. The only question was could he stand the gaff of playing behind an expansionist line?

Saints coach Tom Fears decided to alternate the two quarterbacks in the exhibition season. In the first game against the Rams, Cuozzo started and Kilmer relieved. The Saints lost, but Billy was outstanding in defeat and Fears named him the starter against St. Louis the following week.

As a starter, Bill immediately got the team moving. The line fired out at the snap, and the backs hit the holes, taking Kilmer's crisp handoffs. He was a fine field leader and moved the team well. But it was his passing that surprised everyone. As Y. A. Tittle had said, his passes weren't pretty, but they were getting there and the Saints had a couple of receivers who could hold onto the ball.

On two occasions, his passes found their mark in the end zone for scores and the Saints had a surprising, 23-14, victory. This set the pattern for the remainder of the exhibition season. Kilmer started with the first unit, with Cuozzo relieving. It was becoming apparent that Billy was winning the number one job.

By the end of the exhibition season, the experts couldn't believe their eyes. Bill Kilmer had led the expansionist Saints to five straight victories. In those games he had fired for nine touchdowns, six more than Cuozza. And with the possible exception of the veteran Jim Taylor (who had played his college ball at Louisiana State before starring with the Packers), Kilmer was the most popular player on the new team.

Fears had not yet named his starting quarterback, but most observers were rooting heavily for Kilmer.

"It's the feeling down here that Kilmer ignites the team

when he gets into the game," wrote one newsman. "He's unorthodox and the players believe in him no matter what he tries. This is evident even in practice."

If the exhibition victories were a pipe dream, the regular season turned into a nightmare. Billy opened at quarterback and played steady ball. But the Saints as a whole were making too many mistakes, something not uncommon for new teams. When it really counted, they found victories hard to come by. Three games and three losses, and Billy suddenly found himself on the bench.

"It was hard to take," he confessed. "I knew I could move this type of team better than Gary (Cuozzo), but we were losing and the coach had to see what some of the other guys could do."

Sitting the bench was Bill Kilmer's idea of Hades. It ate him up inside. Cuozzo didn't fare much better and Fears began alternating his signalcallers much as he did in the exhibitions. In the final home game with Atlanta Billy came off the bench in the second half to rally his club to a 27-24 victory over the two-year-old Atlanta Falcons.

He got the starting call again in the final regular season game against the Redskins in Washington. With the pressure on, Billy responded, leading the team as he had in the preseason. He moved his runners well, mixed his plays, and tossed a pair of touchdown passes, one an 80-yarder to rookie Dan Abramowicz. The Saints won it, 30-14, and although he didn't know it at the time, Billy Kilmer had won himself a regular job.

The Saints finished with a 3-11 mark, a realistic figure for a first-year club. As for Billy, he'd had more opportunity than ever before, connecting on 97 of 204 passes for 1,341 yards and six touchdowns. His passing percentage was low at 47.5, but considering the circumstances, no one complained. He also finished as the team's third leading rusher with 142 yards on 20 carries. That's an average of 7.1, although he was running mainly on scrambles and broken plays.

By the following summer, Fears made his decision. He shipped Cuozzo off to Minnesota and told Bill he'd be going with him at quarterback. It marked the first time in his career that Bill Kilmer came to camp knowing he had himself a steady job.

"It's a great feeling to know you've finally got it made," said Bill to reporters. "Because I've had the chance to throw more in the last years, my arm is stronger than ever. Now the receivers know my passes better. There's a certain oneness forming throughout the team.

"We're all aware of the second-year lull like Atlanta experienced (the Falcons went from 3-11 to 1-12-1), but I'd say it's possible for the Saints to win 10 games this season." As usual, Billy was the eternal optimist.

Dave Whitsell, a veteran defensive back who had come to the Saints from the Chicago Bears, was also pleased to see Kilmer tabbed number one, and he told why.

"If Bill Kilmer decided to jump off a building, everyone here would jump with him," Whitsell said. "That's the kind of leader he is.

"I really think he's arrived. In fact, he's just a step away from greatness. I think he'll be the next Bobby Layne. He's got everyone around here thinking like winners. Layne did that, too."

It may have sounded like a lot of talk about a player who hadn't done much on the field. But in an early scrimmage against the San Diego Chargers, Billy showed his critics with a 14-of-22 day, good for 274 yards and three touchdowns. There was no longer much doubt about his ability to handle the T.

Several weeks later the Saints hosted the powerful Cleveland Browns in an exhibition game held before 70,045 fans at the Sugar Bowl in New Orleans. Kilmer turned them on again, connecting on 20 of 33 passes for

261 yards and two scores as the Saints routed the Browns, 40-27.

It wasn't an easy year. There were high points in the regular season, too, but a young team cannot pick up experience overnight. The Saints rolled over the Browns in the 40-27 exhibition, but when it counted during the year, Cleveland prevailed twice, 24-10, and 34-17.

The Saints were in the Century Division of the Eastern Conference during 1968, and, along with Cleveland, were joined by the Cardinals and Steelers. They lost to the Cards twice, but beat the Steelers a pair and actually finished higher than Pittsburgh in the standings. It was a 4-9-1 year for Coach Fears' club.

Billy was good, but not great. He suffered a hairline fracture of the ankle midway through the campaign. He missed the better part of three games—most players would have missed half a season.

There were some heroics for the home fans, but some low moments, too, when the Saints' offensive line couldn't keep the opposition out of the backfield, or when one of Bill's passes was off the mark and intercepted. Yet he still compiled the busiest year of his career, throwing 315 times, completing 167 for 2,060 yards and 15 touchdowns. His passing percentage was over 50, at 53.0, and he was intercepted 17 times.

It's hard to say whether the Saints' fans and management expected miracles, but as Kilmer began leading the team through the 1969 season, a slow chorus of jeers began greeting the quarterback. The jeers increased at each home game. Fans began chanting for a little-known youngster named Edd Hargett, who had played his college ball at Texas A & M.

Yet Kilmer was in the midst of his finest season to date. True, there were some off days, but everyone has off days, and with a three-year-old franchise, it's bound to happen even more.

There was a bad game against Philadelphia in which Bill was yanked out in the middle. But the next week, he went wild against the St. Louis Cardinals. It seemed that every time he got the ball he threw for a touchdown. Cards' QB Charley Johnson was hot, too, and both clubs marched up and down the field all afternoon. When it ended, Kilmer and the Saints had come out on top.

Billy had thrown the ball 32 times, completing 22 for 345 yards and six touchdowns. Johnson also threw for six scores (a record for two quarterbacks in one game), but Billy got one on the ground, also, and his club won, 51-42. It was the Saints' first win of the year.

The victory augured well for the second half of the year, but Billy Kilmer would again have to call on all his courage and guts to continue leading the club.

In a game against his old teammates, the 49ers, Billy suffered a severely separated left shoulder. He led the Saints to another win, 43-38, but after the game the doctors gave him the bad news.

"You need an immediate operation or the injury could lead to a permanent deformity of the shoulder."

"Can I play with it?" Kilmer asked.

"Yes, it won't get worse. But you know the consequences if you delay surgery."

"I'll play," said Kilmer without a moment's hesitation. When you wait as long as Billy Kilmer to be number one, you don't think about consequences.

Doctor Kenneth Saer, the Saints' physician, explained the injury to reporters. "It was a complete separation," said Dr. Saer. "It was the type of injury that required immediate surgery or could produce a painful joint. Without an operation he will have a deformity. His left shoulder will drop down and the clavicle (collar bone) will stick up."

It didn't matter to Kilmer. He continued to play,

despite the painful shoulder and equally painful jeering from the fans.

A few weeks later, Billy started against the Steelers. Pittsburgh went ahead, 14-0, and the fans began chanting, WE WANT HARGETTT! Fears paced the sideline, debating whether to make a change. Suddenly Bill got hot, hitting seven straight passes and culminating the drive with a touchdown strike to end Ray Poage.

At the half, Billy had completed nine of 14 for 148 yards. But the patchwork offensive line had allowed him to be sacked five times for a loss of 56 yards. The Steelers still led at the outset of the fourth quarter, 24-27, and Fears finally sent Hargett into the game. The fickle fans went wild, cheering the youngster as Kilmer walked slowly and sadly to the sideline.

Hargett led a drive downfield. With the ball near the goal line, Kilmer suddenly reentered to a shower of catcalls. Hargett had been shaken up and they wanted Bill's experience near the goal line. Sure enough, he set up the tying score and later the winning field goal. At the end his stats read 15 of 28 for 219 yards. Not bad. Asked about being pulled and the subsequent boos he heard, Bill was slightly angered.

"It's the coach's decision as to who plays and who doesn't. I'm just happy I made a contribution. As for the booing, it doesn't bother me normally, but it did a bit today because I thought I did a pretty good job."

There were additional victories—over the Eagles (26-17), and New York Giants (25-24)—giving the Saints a 5-9 mark and continued improvement, but Billy began feeling his days were numbered.

Statistically, he had his best year, completing 193 of 360 for 2,532 yards and 20 big touchdowns. Yet when the 1970 season opened, he found himself a part-timer, alternating with Hargett. There was increasing talk that the Saints were anxious to draft Mississippi's all-American, Archie Manning, and they were playing as though they wanted that last pick. After three years of progress, the Saints plummeted to a 2-11-1 mark. Wholesale changes were in order.

Billy threw just 237 passes that year, with six touchdowns to his credit against 17 interceptions. The high point of the season came in early November when he led the club to a 19-17 upset of the Detroit Lions, passing to Al Dodd in the closing seconds to set up Tom Dempsey's record-setting 63-yard field goal. But soon after the year was out, word began spreading that Kilmer would be traded.

"I asked out," said Billy, "as soon as they grabbed Manning in the draft. Where to go was another problem. I knew I couldn't go to a team with a youth movement in progress. By the time they were contenders I'd be too old to play anymore. I wanted my chance with a winner, a team ready to make a move on the championship."

The Washington Redskins was not one of those teams. The Skins were perennial losers. They had hired the great Vince Lombardi in 1969 and his coaching expertise and leadership moved the club to a 7-5-2 season. But Lombardi's untimely death set the Skins back and they were 6-8 in 1970. It looked as if they were starting all over again.

Then the Redskin owners signed George Allen, the fine coach of the Rams. Newsmen asked Allen what his building program for the future would be.

"The future is now," he snapped in a now famous statement. "I plan to make changes in this club before the season starts. I want proven players and I'll trade draft choices to get them. No rookie is going to pick up experience at my expense."

Allen was true to his word. He was at the helm a little over two weeks when he made his first deal. He sent a second stringer named Tom Roussel to New Orleans in exchange for Billy Kilmer. Allen told the press that Kilmer was a gutty leader who never quit, the type of player he'd want no matter where he was coaching.

But wait a minute. Didn't the Redskins have a quarterback, a man named Christian Adolph "Sonny" Jurgensen? Right! And wasn't he regarded as one of the greatest passers who ever lived! Right again. While Kilmer was having his big year in 1969, all Jurgy was doing was completing 274 passes in 442 attempts for 3,102 yards, 22 touchdowns, and a completion percentage of 62.0. That's the kind of thrower Sonny was. But he was also 37 years old and Allen wanted insurance.

"I wasn't very happy about going to the Redskins," Kilmer confessed. "There was no way I could step in and beat out Sonny for the starting job. I couldn't see myself as backup again, not at this point. A couple of years as a backup again and people would forget about me. I saw myself on this team, but with my chance—my real chance—never coming."

Bill's fears seemed justified, at least by Allen's other statements immediately following the trade.

"Sonny Jurgensen is still my quarterback," said the coach with finality. "This deal has nothing to do with Sonny's status here. We got Billy as a backup, a backup who could step in and do the job if he has to. When you get a guy like Kilmer it's better than having a draft pick."

Bill did a great deal of soul-searching during the off-season. But he had faith in Allen and there was just one way he could play it. When he reported to camp, he was in shape and ready to go.

During camp, reporters looked for an intense rivalry between the two quarterbacks, and some were surprised when they became fast, close friends. Both QBs looked good in camp, with some saying Kilmer had the edge in moving the team. Then before the first exhibition, Jurgy bruised a thumb and Kilmer started against the San Diego Chargers.

Bill was still learning a new system and didn't look good. The Chargers won the game and one George Allen streak was ended. His teams had never lost in the preseason. Jurgy was healed the next week and he saw most of the action in the ensuing games. When Kilmer did play, he continued to look nervous and unsure, and a familiar chorus of boos began cascading down from the upper reaches of Robert F. Kennedy Stadium in Washington.

Then in the second to last exhibition, the Skins were in Miami facing the Dolphins. Jurgy wasn't having a good game. In the third quarter he tossed one over the middle that was picked off by safety Dick Anderson. An angered Jurgy forgot about an unwritten rule that the quarterback protect himself. He tore after Anderson and blasted through several blockers to help with the tackle. When he got up he was in obvious pain.

Jurgy came slowly to the sideline, his left shoulder slumping lower than his right. A bone in the shoulder had been fractured. Sonny was through for at least eight weeks.

Suddenly and unexpectedly there was another quarterback in the game for Washington. The first time the Skins got the ball he dropped back and rifled a 47-yard scoring pass to Roy Jefferson. Miami won the game, but Bill Kilmer quickly showed his club he was ready to assume leadership.

"When I finished that game," Kilmer recalls, "George called me in just to tell me the job was mine. He wouldn't make any more moves. He also told me how much confidence he had in me. Here's my chance, I thought. Now there'd be no more talking or thinking. I just had to go out there and do it."

To the press, Bill confidently announced, "I can win

and operate as efficiently as Sonny. If I didn't think that way I wouldn't be doing much good for the team."

Many observers agreed. Said one long-time Redskin booster. "Kilmer is perfectly suited for the Redskins. He'll win with them. He controls the game, but unlike Sonny, he doesn't dominate it. He inspires. He relates. And he knows his limitations."

Through several other shrewd deals, Allen had given Kilmer a much-improved team with which to work. The offense was fine, with super-runner Larry Brown and rugged Charley Harraway. Charley Taylor, Roy Jefferson, and Jerry Smith formed a first-rate trio of pass catchers. Both lines and the defensive linebackers and secondary were bolstered by the acquisition of able veterans, some aging, but all experienced and all winners.

The 1971 season opened in St. Louis with the Redskins coming to town as decided underdogs. Billy was deluged with a host of questions, most of them asking how he was going to fill Sonny Jurgensen's shoes.

"I'm not here to fill anyone's shoes," he snapped. "I'm here to follow a game plan and bring us home a winner."

It was a rainy, muddy Sunday as the Skins went up against the Cards. With the slippery football a risk to handle, Bill played it smart, sticking with basic running plays and only throwing occasionally. But one of his passes was a 31-yard touchdown strike to Smith and the Skins went on to win 24-17. Allen said Bill called a "masterful" game and he exhorted the team to continue winning.

Critics said Bill threw just six passes and didn't really prove anything, so a week later he went out and shut some mouths. He did it at the expense of the Giants, in one of the most brilliant passing days of his career. He connected on 23 of 32 attempts for 309 yards. Two of his tosses went for TDs, both to Charley Taylor, one covering 71 yards, the other, two yards. He did it long and he did it short, as the Skins won, 30-3.

Suddenly the booing stopped. When the team came home, Kilmer was treated like a long-lost native son, an instant hero. And he didn't let them down. The next week he engineered a brilliant 20-16 upset of the champion Dallas Cowboys, uncorking a 50-yard scoring toss to Jefferson to break the back of a Dallas rally. With Kilmer at the helm, the Skins had become bonafide contenders.

He made it four in a row the next week, leading his club to a 22-13 win over Houston, and the following Sunday he did it again, spearheading a 20-0 whitewash of St. Louis. The Skins were 5-0 and Billy Kilmer was riding high. Things were going so well with the surprising Redskins that some suggested the team might not be as successful if Jurgensen were playing. But the first to come to Sonny's defense was Bill Kilmer. He'd been there before.

"I say that we'd be doing even better if Sonny were playing. He's a winner who happens to be a fine person and great quarterback."

When someone suggested that Bill was being too modest, he replied promptly. "I'll never get a big head. I know as well as anyone that this kind of success lasts only as long as you win. But I'll say this much. I've never had an offense like this before. It's sensational. Coach Allen is building a club with an amazing amount of spirit. I just love being part of it."

The bubble burst the next week as the Skins fell victim to the tough Kansas City Chiefs, 27-20. After a victory over New Orleans and a surprise 7-7 tie with Philadelphia, Allen's club lost two more to the Bears and Cowboys. The Dallas game ended 13-0, and Kilmer was getting down about his performance.

But the team pulled out just in time. They won two more and then traveled to Los Angeles to face the Rams. Early in the first quarter Kermit Alexander intercepted a

Kilmer aerial and galloped 82 yards for a touchdown return that gave L.A. a 7-0 lead. Right there it looked as if Kilmer and the Skins would fold.

But a few minutes later Kilmer dropped back to pass, totally undaunted by the interception, and whipped a long one down the right sideline to Roy Jefferson. The ball was right on the button, and Jefferson gathered it in and continued on his way to a 70-yard touchdown.

Later in the period Kilmer connected with Clifton McNeil on a 32-yarder, and just before halftime he went for it on a fourth and one, in close, calling on Larry Brown who bulled over to give the Skins a 24-10 halftime lead.

Another TD strike to Jefferson highlighted the second half and when it ended the Redskins had won the game, 38-24. As for Kilmer, he had completed 14 of 19 passes for 246 yards and three touchdowns. Bill played down his performance, but the Associated Press thought enough of it to name him the Offensive Player of the Week.

Cleveland whipped the Skins the final week of the season, but Washington surprised with a 9-4-1 record, the best in 29 years, and entered the playoffs by having the best second-place mark in the NFC. Dallas captured the divisional crown at 11-3.

The first playoff game with San Francisco was a complete disappointment. The Skins fought hard, but were outgunned in the final quarter and beaten, 24-20. It was a double disappointment to Kilmer; the 49ers had been his first team. But the defeat couldn't cloud the Skins' amazing season. Allen himself said, "It was Bill Kilmer who brought us to the playoffs."

And a Washington newsman put Kilmer's performance into an even better perspective.

"Billy Kilmer did his job with a consistency that no one could have possibly predicted. He beat teams with his arm, with his head, and with his guts. He used everything at his command. He played the 1971 season with the candor of a street fighter. He would not lose. He would have to be beaten."

Statistically, Billy completed 166 of 306 passes for 2,221 yards and a 54.2 percentage. He tossed for 13 touchdowns and had an equal number of passes picked off. His teammates voted him Most Valuable Redskin and he finished fourth in the balloting for NFL Player of the Year. He was third in passing among all NFC quarterbacks.

In late January of 1972 Billy Kilmer won another award. He was voted the Most Courageous Athlete of 1971 by the Philadelphia Sports Writers Association. Bill was cited for coming back from his serious leg injury suffered in the auto crash, then overcoming other serious injuries to get the Redskins into the playoffs.

In his acceptance speech, the emotional Kilmer expressed his gratitude, then said he was going to give the award to someone in his family who deserved it more—his 12-year-old daughter, Kathy.

Kathy Kilmer was born with cerebral palsy and disjointed hips, and the little girl had undergone a series of operations to help her walk. When Billy received the award Kathy was facing still another operation and he had her on his mind. He was well aware that there were some things in the world more difficult than facing mammoth onrushing linesmen.

When Billy reported to camp for the 1972 season he still didn't have the secure feeling that many pro quarterbacks enjoy. He had finished a strong number one, but Sonny Jurgensen was back, recovered from his injury, in shape, and ready to battle for his old job. Allen stated publicly that he'd go with the quarterback who had brought the team to the playoffs, but Billy and everyone else knew that if Jurgy was right, he couldn't be denied indefinitely.

Early in the exhibition season the Skins faced the Denver Broncos. Kilmer played the first half, hit six of 17, including a TD to Jefferson. He put 17 points on the scoreboard. Jurgy then took over and did even better, hitting six of seven for 144 yards and two TDs, including a 65-yard bomb to Tommy Mason. He, too, put 17 points on the board, and after the game George Allen said:

"No team in football has two better quarterbacks than we have."

Both continued to impress right through the season opener in Minnesota when Allen, true to his word, started Billy Kilmer.

In a hard-fought struggle from start to finish, the Redskins were outplayed statistically by the Vikings, but did enough things right to win, 24-21. The next week the team came home to face the Cardinals and when Kilmer came out on the field he received a familiar reception—a chorus of boos. It seems the fans felt in their hearts that a healthy Jurgensen should be the team's quarterback. There were even bumper stickers which called for Sonny's reinstatement.

Against the Cards Kilmer had an average game, yet won, 24-10. Now there was a real clamor for Sonny in Washington sports circles. Even Billy was forced to comment on the growing issue.

"Let's face it," he said. "There has to be a clear-cut number one for the team's sake. Sometimes a quarterback sees something in the first half that he knows he can exploit in the second half. You can only get the real tempo of the game by going all the way. I'm sure Sonny would say the same thing."

Game number three was played against the lowly New England Patriots in Foxboro, Massachusetts. Billy was good that day. He threw three scoring passes and just missed a fourth when Jefferson was ruled out of bounds after an apparent touchdown catch. But the Patriots didn't quit and they somehow pushed over a late score to upset the Skins by a point, 24-23. Two days later Sonny Jurgensen was practicing with the first unit.

Like most great quarterbacks, Jurgensen made the most of his opportunity. He led the Skins to two easy victories, showing that his classic passing form hadn't rusted with inactivity. He was hitting better than ever and it began to look as if Kilmer would never get in again. Then the Skins rolled into Yankee Stadium to play the Giants.

Jurgensen started and ran the offense for 13 plays. On the 14th, he called a little rollout to the right, took the snap and about four steps. Suddenly he pulled up lame, hobbling around in pain. Jurgy had ruptured his achilles tendon. Just like that. He walked slowly to the sideline, finished for the season once more. And without warning, Billy Kilmer was on the field, this time to stay.

Rising to the occasion despite his two-week layoff, Billy threw for two scores and Larry Brown rushed for an incredible 191 yards, as the Skins won the game, 23-16.

The next week, Billy showed everyone that he could do the job again. Facing Joe Namath and the New York Jets, Billy threw a 45-yard TD strike to Jefferson, a 70-yard completion to Taylor, setting up another score, and an 89-yard pass-run TD play to Larry Brown. The Skins won, 35-17, with Kilmer the star once again. After the game, Bill told newsmen how Jurgy's injury enabled him to change his style.

"I was throwing a lot stronger today than if Sonny was there behind me. Then I wouldn't take chances. Without him I can gamble because my position is different psychologically. Without him behind me I can freewheel out there and do things without worrying about the coach jerking me. My guys had confidence they could beat them deep and we did.

"It's just a different thing now knowing the job is mine. If Jurgy's there I might hold back and not zip the ball as hard—or maybe even run instead of throwing. But even if I throw an interception now, I stay in. Period."

In the ensuing weeks, Kilmer led the Skins as well as they'd ever been led. He whipped the Giants, 27-13, connecting on 15 of 23 for 256 yards, and he continued to win after that. In the five games that followed his return, Bill threw for 12 touchdowns, completing 54 of 95 passes for 859 yards.

During the same period the Skins were inside their opponents' 20-yard line 11 times. Billy Kilmer took the team in on all 11 occasions. In four of the five games, Billy brought the Skins from behind for the victory.

Kilmer led the club to six straight wins, seven including the Giant game when Jurgy was hurt. With an 11-1 record, the Skins clinched the Eastern Division title in the NFC. With 1,000-yard runner Larry Brown resting some minor injuries in the final two games, and the team already thinking ahead to the playoffs, the Skins dropped a pair and finished at 11-3.

Billy wound up fourth among NFC passers with 120 completions in 225 attempts for a 53.3 percentage and 1,648 yards. He threw for a big 19 touchdowns and had just 11 intercepted. It might not have been his best year statistically, but it had to be his most satisfying artistically.

Yet the season wasn't complete. There were still the playoffs, and the Skins wanted more than anything else to get into the Super Bowl. That was the goal everyone was pointing to.

Before the first-round playoff game against Green Bay, Billy Kilmer talked about the upcoming weeks.

"We've just got to dedicate ourselves, that's all," he said. "Just three weeks is all it will take, but we'll reap the value of that dedication for the rest of our lives."

Kilmer practiced what he preached against the Packers. He was a master of execution. Calling a tight, ball-control game, Billy had the Skins in command from the outset. With the score tied in the second quarter and the ball on the 32, Billy dropped back and lofted a perfect pass in the direction of Jefferson, who grabbed it on the goal line and went in. That made it 10-3, and the foot of Curt Knight gave the Skins the rest. Washington had a 16-3 victory and went into the NFC finals against Dallas.

Kilmer didn't throw much in the Packer game. He was just seven for 14 for 100 yards. But he did what was necessary. Larry Brown had 101 yards rushing and the two kept the Packer defense hopping.

What Kilmer did to the Cowboys the next week no one expected. Before a huge crowd at RFK Stadium, Kilmer and the Skins came out smoking. Billy had one of the most brilliant days of his career. He started it all with a 15-yard TD strike to Taylor in the second quarter, giving his team a 10-3 halftime lead.

Then in the final period he opened up, hitting Taylor with a neat 45-yard scoring pass to put the icing on the cake. Curt Knight had four field goals and the Redskins were NFC champs, 26-3, as their defense completely shut off the Cowboy attack.

Kilmer was 14 for 18, throwing for 194 yards in a display of passing and leadership that had the whole country talking. In the two weeks preceding the Skins Super Bowl clash with Miami, everyone learned the Billy Kilmer story. For the first time in his life he was a national celebrity.

The Super Bowl wouldn't be easy. Miami was bidding to become the first team to march through a pro-football season unbeaten in 17 games. They'd already won 16, the first 14 in the regular season and two more in the play-offs. Coach Don Shula had a well-balanced, deep, talented team. They seldom made mistakes, and they never let an opponent's mistake get by them.

The Dolphins feared the Skins and their tandem of Bill

Kilmer and Larry Brown. Both had been spectacular in the Packer and Cowboy games.

"Billy Kilmer is what the Washington Redskins are all about," one newspaper story began. Another claimed that in reality Allen preferred Billy at quarterback to Jurgensen because of the way Kilmer stuck to a game plan and just chipped away at the opposition until they crumbled.

That's what he tried to do against the Dolphins. Playing in the Los Angeles Coliseum, where he had seen his first game so many years before, Kilmer tried to repeat his tactics of the other playoff games. He began by trying to establish his running game. It wasn't working. The stout Miami line was wrapping up Larry Brown before he could get started.

So Billy tried some short passes. He only had to throw a couple before he realized something. "I wasn't sharp. I wasn't throwing the ball well." And the Skins weren't moving.

Meanwhile, Miami quarterback Bob Griese was moving his team. In the first period he hit on six straight passes. The fourth pass was a 28-yarder to Howard Twilley that wound up in the end zone for a score. The kick made it 7-0.

The Skins tried to bounce back. Kilmer looked for Larry Brown midway in the second period, but middle linebacker Nick Buoniconti picked the ball off and returned it 32 yards. From there, the Dolphins drove in on the ground, Jim Kiick taking it over, and Miami had a 14-0 halftime lead.

The Skins worked desperately to score. But there was no running game and the Miami zone was laying for Kilmer. One time when Billy had Jerry Smith wide open in the end zone his pass hit the goal post and bounced away.

Not until late in the fourth quarter did the Skins score. And that was on a freak play. The Dolphins were trying a field goal, and a bad pass from center fouled the play.

Cornerback Mike Bass picked up the football and raced it into the end zone. That made it 14-7, but there was next to no time left. Miami ran out the clock before the Skins could get the ball back.

It was a tremendous disappointment for everyone. Kilmer himself took the blame, saying he should have passed better. Maybe. But there was no running game to support him. Larry Brown had just 26 yards and that put the pressure on Kilmer. He was 14 for 26 but couldn't connect on the big ones or on the bombs. The Dolphin zone bottled him up.

Allen defended his quarterback. "He got us there," the coach said bluntly, and there was surely a bundle of truth in that statement. Kilmer had been the driving force of the Skins attack ever since Jurgensen limped off the Yankee Stadium turf so many weeks before. Brown, Taylor, Harraway, Jefferson, and many of the other Redskins had outstanding years, but it was the spirit and leadership of Billy Kilmer that could be singled out.

That leadership was still in evidence in 1973, though it was another season of torment for Billy. He ought to be used to it by now. The Skins came back with their two veterans, Kilmer and Jurgensen, but before long Sonny was having knee trouble and Billy stomach problems. The club was also having problems generating the usual running game, putting even more pressure on the quarterbacks.

Billy's problem was an intestinal disorder, a blockage that would need surgery after the season. Yet he played out the season and had an outstanding campaign under the circumstances, completing 122 of 227 passes for 1,656 yards. He threw 14 TDs and had only nine intercepts.

The Skins weren't quite as potent as the year before, but still finished with a 10-4 mark, tied with Dallas for the divisional title. Dallas had the top spot in the playoffs because of a point advantage and the Skins, as the wild-card team, had to face the Minnesota Vikings.

In the week before the playoff game Billy Kilmer was in the hospital, being fed through tubes, his stomach problem worsening. He couldn't practice, but he was out there at game time calling the signals.

He led his team coolly and well. The Skins had a 7-3 lead at the half and it was 10-10 after three. Then Fran Tarkenton found his wide receiver John Gilliam on two straight scoring passes to give the Vikes the lead. Playing in pain and with shortness of breath, Kilmer tried to lead the Skins back.

With time running out he drove the club downfield, faded back, and hit Roy Jefferson with a 28-yard TD pass, making the score 27-20. He kept throwing for the tie the final time he had the ball, but the Vikes used a prevent defense and stopped him.

"The real hero of this game was Billy Kilmer," said winning quarterback Fran Tarkenton. "He played when most guys would be in the hospital and he played brilliantly. I can't think of too many other guys who could have done what he did under those conditions."

Where to now? Despite his obvious success and the admiration earned through 1973, Billy wasn't assured of a starting job, maybe not even a job in 1974. Jurgensen was back again, and this time the wily Coach Allen brought in a youngster. He was Joe Theismann, a former star at Notre Dame, who had been quarterbacking in Canada for two years. He was already being touted as a Redskin QB of the future.

But with Allen, the future is always now, and in 1974, a familiar script developed. Kilmer, then Jurgensen, then Kilmer again, quarterbacked the Skins. It was the hot man or the healthy man who got the call. And with two vets, you never know which one is going to be healthy.

At any rate, both performed well, getting the Skins

back into the playoffs, where, as in years past, they were eliminated.

Yet both old quarterbacks had fine years. Kilmer saw more action, hitting on 137 of 234 passes for 1,632 yards and a 58.5 percentage. He had 10 TD passes and six interceptions. Sonny, despite injuries, still had a rifle arm. He was 107 for 167, a fantastic 64.1 percentage. And he threw for 11 TDs. The twosome gave the Skins the best passing attack in the league.

But as 1975 approached, each would be a year older. Now Allen made another move. He signed former NFLer Randy Johnson, who had been playing in the World Football League. That made four quarterbacks, and that was even too many for the insurance-conscious Allen. The question was, which would go? And where?

Kilmer and Jurgensen were friendly competitors. Neither was ever jealous of the other. It was a unique football relationship.

"Sonny and I have a great relationship," said Billy. "I've been on teams where there has been animosity between two quarterbacks. But Sonny and I have become friends. We're roommates on the road and we root for each other. And all we want to do is win. To tell the truth, if we were different, we could have split this team apart. But I think we've really helped with our attitude toward each other."

They were not immune from fan criticism, though. In the 1974 playoff loss to the Rams, many criticized Allen for starting Kilmer and not Jurgy. But as the coach had said so often, "Billy Kilmer is the man most responsible for getting us into the playoffs four straight years. I don't have to make any excuses or apologies for him."

Yet in the off-season Billy and the Skins had their first impasse. The move to obtain Randy Johnson made Billy think that his days as a Redskin were numbered. Jurgensen, despite being almost 41, was a Washington fixture.

And now there were two young QBs. So Billy began talking openly about being traded.

Speculation grew, and in early May of 1975, Billy told the press he had actually been traded but the deal had been called off at the last second. The reason was that Allen suddenly decided that it was Sonny Jurgensen who had to go. Sonny, with his big salary and bad legs, was a luxury the Skins could no longer afford. So he was, in essence, "retired" by the Redskins. In other words, he was forced out. So Kilmer would stay, but the treatment accorded his friend Jurgensen still angered him, and he continued to hint that he, too, might be better off playing somewhere else.

"I hated the way Sonny had to go out," he said. "He deserved better. I think he could have played some more. Heck, he led the NFC in passing last year. But I guess they want to move Thiesmann and Johnson in."

Not exactly. George Allen was still telling people that Billy Kilmer was his quarterback.

"We knew that Sonny couldn't go 14 games anymore. Kilmer can, and right now he's our number one."

In late May there was a special early training camp for veterans. For two days Billy didn't show, increasing speculation that something was up. Finally he arrived, and everyone, including Coach Allen, heaved a sigh of relief.

"It makes me smile to see the old pro back," said the coach. "With the type of guy Billy is, we're not going to have any problems. We need him and he needs us."

Billy also tried to mend some fences. "I really want to be part of this team. The guys are super football players and I think we can have a great season."

So when the 1975 season opened, old red-faced number 17 was again at the helm of the Redskin attack. People were saying that Billy looked better than ever, that his passes were even losing some of that wobble.

"Naw," laughed Billy, "I'll always have the wobble. My hands and fingers are too small to throw those pretty spirals."

Spirals or not, Billy was still a winner. In a big game against Dallas he threw several interceptions. As was sometimes the case, the big crowd at RFK Stadium in Washington began booing him mercilessly. But Allen kept him in there. Dallas led, 24-17, late in the fourth quarter and it looked bad. But Billy wouldn't quit. He threw a 60-yard TD strike to tie the game, then drove his club to the winning score in sudden death overtime. When it ended, Coach Allen gave Billy the game ball.

"I've never been booed by bigger crowds than this," Billy said. "I don't blame them. I threw four intercepts and the last might have won it for them. But what a game! Games like this are good for everyone. The fans, the players, the coaches."

So Billy didn't mind the booing. But Skins defensive tackle, the outspoken Diron Talbert, did object.

"The way Kilmer came back and moved the ball club at the end of the game shows what he's made of. I'll tell you this, I was embarrassed for just about everyone of our fans today. They owe Kilmer an apology."

Billy didn't need one. The next week he led the Skins past the Browns, 23-7, hitting on 15 of 33 for 207 yards and two scores. But after that things started going sour for the Skins. They were involved in several overtime games. One against the Cards they lost on a controversial call. In several others the opposing team just scored first. They were in a real battle with St. Louis and Dallas for a playoff spot.

And, as usual, Billy was getting banged up. First there was a slight shoulder separation in a game against the Giants. But he came back to hit on 13 of 25 for 233 yards and three scores in a brilliant 31-30 victory over the Vikings. Billy led the Skins on a 77-yard drive in the closing minutes of play, capping it with a 15-yard TD toss to Frank Grant.

But shortly after that Billy suffered a broken bone behind his little toe. Now he had to play with a special harness on his foot. But playing with pain was an old story to Kilmer, and as the Skins approached a crucial showdown game with Dallas, the Cowboy coach, Tom Landry, was full of praise for the Washington veteran.

"Billy Kilmer is the best play-action passer in football today," said Landry. "He's great at throwing through people and by people. That's their great strength—you've got to be able to control the play-action passes to do any good."

The Cowboys were able to contain Billy. They were ahead, 17-10, in the third period, if that's containing him, when linebacker D.D. Lewis hit Billy from the blind side. His shoulder was banged up badly this time, and he was forced from the game. The Cowboys went on to win, 31-10, eliminating the Skins from the playoffs for the first time in five years.

After the game, Coach Allen had nothing but praise for his quarterback, who now had to face still another operation and would miss the final game of the year.

"Billy Kilmer has done a great job in every aspect," said Allen. "He's had the best year he has ever had. It's a shame we're not in the playoffs for him."

It was a great year. Billy hit on 178 of 346 passes for 2,440 yards. He was second in the league with 23 TD passes and had just 16 picked off. For an old man, that's pretty good chuckin'.

And once again people were talking about the raw courage and guts of Billy Kilmer. Phil Tuckett, who did a film on Billy for the NFL, talked about the experience.

"The thing about Kilmer is that he is so vulnerable," said Tuckett. "And it always shows in his face. He wears a different kind of bar on his helmet so that his expression always shows."

"The big thing in football now is to acquire a stoical mask. A mask that hides your feelings. But Kilmer's so different. If he's happy, you see it; if he's hurt, you see it. He just shows on every play that he's so human."

During the off-season Billy once again went under the knife. In fact, he had a dual operation, to correct both his shoulder and foot problems at the same time. Since it was his right shoulder there would be a question about his throwing until the new season started.

As usual, George Allen did some wheeling and dealing in the off-season. He signed a couple of high-priced free agents, running backs John Riggins and Calvin Hill, as well as tight end Jean Fugett. But he didn't make any moves at quarterback. The job still belonged to Kilmer, with the anxious Joe Theismann waiting in the wings.

The 1976 season was much like '75 for Kilmer and the Skins. There was a bevy of close games, some wins and some losses. A playoff spot was always in question. Billy started well, then began to get banged up. In one game Theismann started and threw for more than 300 yards. Once more, everyone wrote Kilmer off. Allen, indeed, did start Theismann for a couple of more games, but the youngster faltered. With the playoffs on the line the coach turned back to Kilmer.

Finally it came down to the last game. The Skins had to defeat the Cowboys to clinch a wild-card spot. Dallas had already sewed up the divisional crown. But unless the Skins won, the St. Louis Cardinals would be the wild-card team.

The pressure was really on Billy. The Skins' offense hadn't been perking in recent weeks. Defense dominated the first half on both sides. Dallas had a 7-3 lead with little time left in the half. But then Billy went to work. He drove the Skins 52 yards in just 55 seconds, completing key passes to Mike Thomas, Frank Grant, and Fugett. Finally he hit Fugett for the score from six yards out. At the half the Skins led, 10-7.

But the Cowboys bounced back for a 14-10 lead. A Washington field goal made it 14-13. Billy completed two key passes on that drive. Then in the fourth period Billy got his club moving again. Finally it came to a big third-down play on the Dallas 38. The Cowboys got ready for a big rush.

Billy took the snap and rolled to his right. He fired downfield and hit halfback Thomas for a 34-yard gain to the four. It was the key play of the game. Two plays later Calvin Hill scored the go-ahead TD. The Skins got an insurance score on an interception late in the game. They had won it, 27-14, to make the playoffs. Billy was 14 for 30 for 174 yards, and as usual, he was great in the clutch. Once again he was the key man in getting the Skins to the playoffs.

Billy's seasonal status reflected his year. He completed 108 of 206 passes for 1,252 yards and a 52.4 percentage. He threw for 12 scores and had 10 picked off. It was a good year in spite of everything.

Unfortunately the magic once again faded in the playoffs. The Skins ran into a hot Vikings team and were beaten badly. The Vikes won, 35-20. Billy didn't have a great day, but no one blamed him. The Skins are an aging team, with too many holes now. The defense broke down more than the offense.

Of course, it wouldn't be a season if Billy didn't go home with his future in doubt. There was even talk of retirement. But it's hard to see a gutty guy like Billy going out just yet. The Skins still need him, even if he can't play all 14 games.

Billy Kilmer once said that he never plans ahead. He's seen too many hopes, too many dreams dashed by some unforeseen occurrence. "Out of season I've never been a game-play type of guy," is the way he put it.

No, he doesn't waste time looking for trouble. But no matter what the future brings, Billy Kilmer has proved time and again that he's ready to face anything.

# ★ TERRY BRADSHAW ★

★ It was a warm spring day in 1966. The Shreveport Woodlawn High School track team was engaged in a meet with a rival Louisiana school. The main body of the teams as well as most of the spectators were gathered around the oval track, watching the running and jumping events. Off in a far corner of the sprawling field a small group of people gathered for the javelin event.

The young competitors began hurling the spear for distance. Up stepped Shreveport Woodlawn's top thrower, a tall, lanky blond youth with a tough-looking, wiry build. He carefully adjusted his grip on the javelin, then stared straight ahead for a moment before starting his approach.

The big youngster ran with strong, powerful strides. As he neared the take-off line, he went into the final crossover and skip that characterizes perfect javelin form, then released the spear with a loud grunt.

All eyes followed the blue blur and it shot off his arm like a rocket. It seemed to keep rising as if jet propelled.

When the other boys' throws began descending, this youngster's was still flying upward and outward. Finally, it began to arc downward. When it hit, its point buried deep in the ground so there could be no mistaking the spot.

Meet officials ran toward the fallen spear. They had not been standing out that far. Now they were excited. A tape measure was brought out. The distance was called off. They got another tape and measured again. Once more the distance was shouted out. Everyone began murmuring excitedly.

"Great toss, Terry."

"Way to chuck that thing, Ter."

"That showed 'em, Terry."

But even in the excitement of the explosive throw, no one quite realized exactly what happened. Terry Bradshaw had just broken the national prep school all-time javelin record with a toss of 244 feet, 11 inches. It beat the old mark by more than 13 feet.

Terry's teammates congratulated him and slapped him on the back. It was the first time that Terry Bradshaw's arm had brought him nationwide recognition, but it wouldn't be the last. Terry could have continued with the javelin and perhaps have become a world-class thrower. But he decided to concentrate on throwing something else, an oblong-shaped sphere made out of pigskin—a football.

Four years later, the same Terry Bradshaw would capture the national spotlight once again. And this time people other than a handful of track enthusiasts would know who he was. For in that span of time, Terry Bradshaw had honed his football talents to such a fine degree that he became the most talked about pro football quarterback prospect since Joe Namath.

In Terry's case, it was a remarkable feat. While the likes of Namath, Fran Tarkenton, Billy Kilmer and later

Jim Plunkett developed their football skills at great universities like Alabama, Georgia, UCLA, and Stanford, Terry Bradshaw got his gridiron baptism at Louisiana Polytechnic Institute.

What's that, you ask? Well, it's a relatively small university (student body about 8,000) located in Ruston, Louisiana. It plays its football in the Gulf States Conference against such teams as McNeese State, Lamar Tech, the University of Southwest Louisiana, and Northeast Louisiana State. The rest of the slate is similarly unexciting, except to football fans of the region and some footloose pro scouts.

Anyway, that's where Bradshaw played, but it wasn't long before the power attached to his right shoulder began speaking for itself. Anyone with an arm like Terry Bradshaw's would have attracted attention even if he played in no league at all.

A modern version of Jack Armstrong, the All-American boy, Terry was devoutly religious, clean-cut, and clean-living. He seemed to have the world at his feet when he broke a host of passing records at Louisiana Tech. Pro scouts were drooling, pro coaches dreaming ... when they weren't scheming about ways to get him. With his bright blond hair and handsome face, he was truly a Golden Boy with a golden future.

Bradshaw said he was happy when the Pittsburgh Steelers drafted him, a team that had a 1-13 record the year before he got there. An impressive exhibition season solidified Terry's immediate claim to superstardom. The fans said that his release was quicker then Namath's, that he ran better than Tarkenton, that he was stronger than Gabriel. Perhaps no rookie quarterback in the history of the game has ever had so many words of praise heaped upon him at one time. But then the 1970 season started, and with it the most trying time of Terry Bradshaw's young life.

That life began on September 12, 1948, in Shreveport, Louisiana. Terry was the second of three sons born to Mr. and Mrs. W. M. (Bill) Bradshaw. When Terry was just a toddler, his family made a big move, going to Clinton, Iowa, where Mr. Bradshaw had taken a new job. Terry went through his early grammar school days there.

The Bradshaws remained in Iowa for a few years; then Mr. Bradshaw announced that he was taking the family back to Shreveport, where he became plant manager for the American Machine and Foundry Corporation. Years afterward, Mr. Bradshaw told why he did it:

"One reason I came back was because of sports. I wanted the boys to participate and I knew that Shreveport had a superior junior sports program."

Yet Bill Bradshaw adds a note of caution, lest someone misunderstand his intentions. "I never insisted my boys become athletes," he said frankly. "I hoped they'd be ballplayers, I exposed them to it and I encouraged them. But no one can force a boy into being something he doesn't have a real feeling for."

Terry's older brother, Gary, just a year his senior, was also a fine football prospect until a fall from a tree injured his back permanently. Craig, the youngest, is still only 15 years old. He has a possible future in baseball.

Bill Bradshaw was a sports lover from way back. When he was a kid he hung around with Joe Adcock (later the first baseman with the Milwaukee Braves) and the two were well-known figures on the Louisiana sandlots. When the Pittsburgh Steelers came to Shreveport for an exhibition game in 1952, somehow Bill Bradshaw ended up driving their team bus out to the field. "They gave me $20 for that little ride," he recalls. "The most I ever got from other teams in those days was five dollars, so I've always maintained that the Steelers couldn't be a cheap outfit."

Of course, Bill Bradshaw had no way of knowing that

his son would someday be negotiating with that same team, talking turkey at a figure considerably higher than the tip the elder Bradshaw received.

But despite his long association with sports and athletes, Bill Bradshaw was above all a devoted family man. A teetotaller and regular churchgoer, Mr. Bradshaw had always believed in family togetherness. The whole family often participated in after-dinner softball games.

"I always believed in keeping my boys busy," Mr. Bradshaw says, "either with sports or chores. That way, they wouldn't have time to get into trouble. In that respect, I guess I've been a strict father, but I don't feel I've been unreasonable, even though I always rode hard herd on the boys."

Mr. Bradshaw stuck by a set of firm rules. There were school night curfews for the boys, no smoking or drinking, respect for all elders, and no automobiles.

"I always had to know where my boys were," Mr. Bradshaw said, "and you don't know where in the world they are if they're running off in cars."

Though Mr. Bradshaw may seem tough and old-fashioned by today's standards, he stuck to his principles and his boys respected him for it. Right to this day, Terry has no complaints about his home life. In fact, he looks to the love and attention he had as a youth as one of the reasons for his success.

Terry's athletic career began slowly and quietly, but there were enough highlights along the way to indicate that there was something special about this bright youngster. When he was living in Clinton, Iowa, as a nine-year-old, he was picked by the coaches of the Little League to join an all-star team which was set to travel to New York. But Terry's joy quickly turned to disappointment when it was discovered that the boys had to be at least ten to make the trip.

When he was 13, he went to visit his grandmother in

Coushatta, Louisiana, for two weeks. During that time he joined a local baseball team and promptly went out and pitched a perfect game. Even then he had the beginnings of that incredible arm.

By the time he entered junior high in Shreveport as a seventh grader, he was ready to play football. But he was small for his age and the coaches wouldn't even issue him a uniform. The next year he was bigger, but there were so many boys with experience that the team again ran out of uniforms before getting around to him.

It was a bitter disappointment for the youngster, but his father advised him not to give up, to believe in himself and keep at it. Then one day he and another youngster who didn't make the team were watching practice. Terry picked up an extra football and began throwing it to the other boy.

"I could throw pretty well, even then," he recalls, "and I told my friend to go out for some long ones. We threw for about 10 minutes or so and I guess the coaches noticed me, because the next day they gave me a uniform."

But that didn't mean they gave him the quarterback job. They made him a linebacker. "I loved it," says Terry now. "I remember one scrimmage when I really felt good. I think I must have made about a dozen unassisted tackles. I figured I had it made. But about a week later I broke my collarbone and missed the whole season."

The injury jinx continued to plague him. The next year, his last at Oak Terrace Junior High, the coaches made him the tailback in a shotgun-type offense, but he separated his shoulder before the first game and didn't return until the final two contests of the season.

"I threw about 50 passes in those two games," he remembers, "and didn't complete a whole lot, but it was a start."

When he arrived at Shreveport Woodlawn High the next year he was just starting to really grow. "I had a hard time convincing my Woodlawn coaches that I could play varsity ball," he says. "They thought I was too small at first, and even when I started growing I guess they still thought of me as a little guy. I rotated between the varsity and junior varsity in both my sophomore and junior seasons. I think I played in maybe three games with the varsity as a junior. They had a senior quarterback that year, Trey Prather (who later went to LSU and subsequently lost his life in Vietnam), who was breaking all the school passing records, and the coaches let him play as much as they could."

By the time he was a senior Terry could be denied no longer. What's more, the team had just one starter back and had to rebuild. Terry became the quarterback and immediately began firing bullet passes all over the field. With him at the helm, the Woodlawn Knights were winners again, taking the district championship and going all the way to the state finals before losing a tough one to Sulphur High, 12-9.

Terry was a dedicated football player by then, and knew he wanted to concentrate on the sport in college. He came home one day shortly after the season ended and told his father that he was going to forget about track that spring. Bill Bradshaw didn't like to hear that. Terry's arm had been getting stronger all the time and he was beginning to make his mark as a javelin thrower.

"There were two reasons why I wanted him to stick with it," says Mr. Bradshaw. "Naturally, I wanted him busy, but I also felt he had the ability to break the state record in the javelin and I wanted him to fulfill that potential. I asked him to stay on the team, to get that record for me. And that's the only time I ever asked one of my boys to actually do something for me. Terry was a good kid and he agreed."

In the second meet of the season, Terry tossed the spear 222 feet. That throw broke the state record his father had asked him to aim for. And, of course, he didn't stop there. Several weeks later at Bossier City he got off the big one, the toss of 244 feet, 11 inches that broke the national prep school all-time javelin record.

"I could have had a track scholarship to almost any school in the country, but I knew then that it was time to concentrate on football."

The next problem was picking a college. The track offers were still much more numerous than the football feelers and Terry did not have very many schools to choose from. Finally, he narrowed it down to three schools, Baylor, Louisiana State University, and Louisiana Tech. The first two are big-time outfits where he could surely achieve national recognition. But there was something about Baylor he didn't like (some said it was the sight of whisky bottles in many of the dormitory rooms), and things never worked out with LSU.

In fact, it was because the LSU people hemmed and hawed for so long that he finally decided on Tech, which was located some 70 miles from his home in Shreveport.

"As far as I'm concerned," Terry said in answering critics who felt he had made a mistake, "Tech plays a real good brand of football. They have a fine coaching staff, use a pro-style offense, and are playing in a new 25,000-seat stadium. If I'm good enough to play pro ball I'll get my chance, no matter which college I attend."

It didn't take Terry long to find admirers. He was just a freshman when a scout saw him for the first time. The man's name was Jim Palmer, and he worked for an organization called BLESTO-V a talent scouting service which worked collectively for the Bears, Lions, Eagles, Steelers, and Vikings.

Anyway, Palmer watched the youngster throw a football for the first time and quickly filled out a report which read in part, "He has the best arm I've ever seen on a freshman quarterback."

Palmer returned in May, when Terry was in the midst of spring practice with the varsity. He was still a freshman, but the scout was already looking to next year. "This youngster has the quickest delivery and strongest arm I've ever seen on a sophomore." Then he added a negative note. "He doesn't scramble well and needs experience." What did anyone expect? Terry was still green behind the ears, though he had seen some varsity action as a frosh.

The club was young and inexperienced itself. Terry was the number two quarterback but didn't really see much action as a frosh in 1966. He was in long enough to throw 81 passes, completing 34 for a 42.0 percentage and 404 yards. He failed to throw a TD pass, however, and had three picked off. The club's 1-9 record and 83 points scored indicated its entire caliber of play.

After the season, Joe Aillet, Tech's coach of 26 years, retired, and Maxie Lambright took his place. Also coming with Lambright as an assistant was Mickey Slaughter, a former Tech signalcaller who played four years with the Denver Broncos of the American Football League. Terry always gives Slaughter much of the credit for his development.

"I built up my arm by lifting weights," he said, "a lot of weights. And plenty of throwing helped me, too. But, basically, it was Coach Slaughter who made me mentally tough. I may have had the physical ability when I first came to Tech, but I didn't have the confidence needed to make an offense go. Someone had to give me the drive and that's what Coach Slaughter did. He drove the confidence into me."

The confidence didn't come overnight. Terry was an alternate quarterback his sophomore year of 1967, as the team began rebuilding under Coach Lambright. The Bulldogs had a couple of big wins, 34-7 over Delta State, and 41-31 against Lamar Tech. But there were losses, too, including a season-ending 58-7 rout at the hands of Southern Mississippi. When it ended, the Bulldogs were 3-7. All they could do was hope their young players would come of age in '68.

As for Terry, he began to show the passing form that was to make him a national celebrity in less than two years. He threw the football 139 times, completing 78 for 981 yards and a 56.1 percentage. He fired his first three touchdown passes, but on the other side had 10 picked off. He still had to learn when to run and when to eat the ball.

When Terry returned for his junior year of 1968 he finally knew the quarterback job was his. He'd be calling the plays and running the Bulldog offense. And it wasn't long before he opened up. He was 13 for 30 and 216 yards in an opening victory over Mississippi State, 20-13. The next week he was a conservative, hitting on just eight of 15 for 105 yards and a score, as Tech whipped East Carolina, 35-7.

Then in the following two weeks, Terry really began putting on an aerial show. He was 20 of 38 for 319 yards and three scores against McNeese State, and then made the fans' eyes pop with a scintillating 28 of 47 for 432 yards and two scores against Southwestern Louisiana. Unfortunately, the Bulldog defense wasn't equal to the task, and Tech lost both games, 27-20 and 28-24. So when the club faced Northwestern State the following week, they were determined not to lose another.

"We figured the success of our season hinged on that game," said Terry. "Some people were calling us chokers, and rapping the defense. But let's face it, it's a team effort and everyone's to blame for a loss."

It was the 53rd meeting between the two teams, so if anyone is wondering how long these small Louisiana schools have been playing the grid game, there's the answer. Anyway, it was a wild contest all the way. Northwestern dominated the first half as Terry could complete just two of 12 passes in a performance that had people shaking their heads. It was a 19-7 game at the half and the Bulldogs looked like they were going down to a third straight defeat.

But in the third period, Terry began hitting. He found Tommy Spinks open for passes of 10 and 13 yards, then rocketed one to Larry Brewer in the end zone for a score. Northwestern upped its lead to 26-14 before Tech drove downfield again, with long runs by its halfbacks. Terry then took it over from the one and the kick made it 26-21. Another Tech score minutes later made it a 28-26 game, with the Bulldogs out in front once again.

Terry got a third TD on a sneak, but the Tech defense again weakened. The Demons scored twice to go ahead by 39-35 with less than three minutes left. Tech got the ball and Terry tried to start another drive. But when he tried a pass over the middle it was picked off by a State defender. With just 2:42 left in the game, it seemed that State had won.

Only this time the Bulldog defense held, and Northwestern was forced to punt. The kick by Larry Smith was returned a few yards to the Tech 18 by Butch Danile. Bradshaw re-entered the game with his team 82 yards from paydirt and just 25 seconds remaining. There was time for one play, perhaps two.

Terry took the snap and dropped straight back. Northwestern had its linemen charging and Bradshaw knew he didn't have much time. He waited until the last possible second, then fired hard and long over the middle. Flanker Ken Liberto ran under the ball at the Demon 40 and suddenly was in the clear, racing all the way to the end zone to complete the dramatic, 82-yard play. Louisiana Tech had won, 42-39.

As for Terry, he had returned from a disastrous first half to complete 11 of 15 second-half passes in leading his team to a great win. And the game turned the season around just as Terry had said it would. Tech went on to take its final five games. The Bulldogs finished with an 8-2 mark and the Gulf States Conference title.

Terry Bradshaw had rewritten the Bulldog record book. During 1968 he completed 176 of 339 passes for a whopping 2,890 yards. His completion percentage was 51.9 and he rifled 22 touchdown passes to his waiting receivers. Just 15 of his throws were intercepted.

The season wasn't yet over for Terry and the Bulldogs. Their fine record earned them a bid to the Grantland Rice Bowl against Akron University. While the game didn't compare in glamor or importance to the Rose or Orange Bowls, both teams were nevertheless ready to give it everything they had.

It was a cold December 14 when the two clubs met at Murfreesboro, Tennessee, but it didn't take long for Terry Bradshaw to warm up the air with his passing.

The Bulldogs began driving as soon as they got the ball. Bradshaw took them downfield by mixing his throwing with running plays and keepers. With the ball on the 16 he dropped back, then took off and scrambled by several Akron players for the score.

Minutes later he struck again, hitting Tommy Spinks with a 36-yard scoring pass, and before the quarter ended, Buster Herren banged over from the two, giving Tech a 21-0 lead.

Akron came back with touchdowns in the second and third quarters, making it 21-13, but in the final period Terry began hitting again, culminating one drive with a six-yard pass to Larry Brewer, and a second by scrambling over himself from the eight. Witnesses claim that he completed one pass after being hit by six different Akron players, with three still hanging onto him when he threw.

The final score was 33-13, and Terry Bradshaw won

the Most Valuable Player Award hands down. He had completed 19 of 33 passes for 261 yards and two scores. In addition, he gained 71 yards on 12 running plays, though that statistic was modified by 36 yards lost trying to pass. But when he ran, he did it well.

After the bowl game Terry could sit back and watch the honors roll in. And there were many. He was the Player of the Year in the Gulf States Conference; the Most Valuable Player at Louisiana Tech; a first team all-America selection by the American Football Coaches Association; the Athlete of the Year in the Gulf States Conference as voted by the Louisiana Sports Writers Association.

That wasn't all. By the end of his junior year, Terry Bradshaw had become one of the most heavily scouted quarterback prospects in the country. At 6-3, 215 pounds, he had the size and strength to play in the pros, and no one ever questioned the quality of his arm.

When Terry returned for his senior year, it was like an anticlimax. What more could he do for an encore? He was already NCAA college division total offense leader (2,987 yards in 426 plays).

And once the season opened, his opponents knew that success hadn't gone to Terry Bradshaw's head. He took up right where he left off—pitching strikes. Three TDs against East Carolina highlighted the opening win (final score: 24-6) and that was just the beginning.

In the third game against Southwestern Louisiana, Terry hit 15 of 25 for 207 yards and ran for another 68 on 10 tries to highlight an easy victory. Then in the fifth game against Chattanooga, Terry played barely one half, hitting nine of 10 for 209 big yards and three TDs. In fact, the stadium transformers failed and the game had to be halted for some 88 minutes. Some joked that it was Bradshaw's lightning that shortcircuited the lights. One pro scout on hand, John Carson of the Eagles, was really impressed by Terry's cool that night.

"I watched him throw a 20-yard touchdown pass and then all the lights went out," Carson said. "The place was dark for almost an hour and a half. When the lights came on again, Bradshaw came back onto the field and threw a 76-yard touchdown pass on the very first play. I couldn't believe how cool he was about it."

The whole season was cool. Tech lost just once, a 24-23 squeaker at the hands of Southern Mississippi. Included in their fine 8-1 record was a smashing 77-40 triumph over Lamar Tech, which broke several school and conference marks. Terry was 17 of 33 in that one, for a big 316 yards. The team returned to the Grantland Rice Bowl again in 1969, this time facing East Tennessee. That one was a mild upset. East Tennessee defenders overwhelmed the Bulldog lines and rapped Terry 12 times for 143 yards in losses. He still managed to complete 20 of 39 for 299 yards, but Tech lost, 34-14.

Thus ended the college career of Terry Bradshaw. He wasn't quite as busy his senior year. Many games were won early and he managed some bench time. He nevertheless completed 136 of 248 for 2,314 yards and 14 scores. That gave him a career total of 463 completions in 879 attempts for a mammoth total of 7,149 yards. His passing percentage for four years was 52.7, and he fired away for 42 touchdowns.

This time his all-America honors weren't restricted to the small college division—although he copped all the top prizes in that division. He was a first-team selection of the American Coaches Association and *Time* Magazine, and made the second team in the *Sporting News* poll. And, of course, he was once again Gulf States Conference Athlete of the Year.

The stage seemed set for a first-round draft. But just to show that he could play with the big boys, Terry accepted invitations to participate in The North-South Game and then in the Senior Bowl game, both post-season affairs that always attract the top college players and pro prospects in the country.

Terry journeyed to Miami for the North-South game that was set for Christmas Day. Mike Phipps was slated to start for the North team, and Terry would be battling Florida State's Bill Cappleman for the starting job on the South Side. The South's coach was Bill Peterson of Florida State, and that gave Terry an early line on just who the starter would be.

The scouts watched the practice sessions intently. When it began to look as if Cappleman would start for the South, Ace Parker of Duke, one of the BLESTO-V scouts, commented, "Look at Bradshaw's delivery! He's really impressive. Cappleman isn't nearly as quick as he is."

Another interested spectator at Miami was Chuck Noll, the youthful coach of the Pittsburgh Steelers. Pittsburgh had just completed a dreadful 1-13 season, the same as the Chicago Bears, and the two teams flipped a coin to see which would get the number one draft choice. The Steelers won. That meant Chuck Noll had a lot of quick decisions to make.

First of all, he wasn't sure if he wanted to draft a quarterback. He had played a rookie in 1969, Terry Hanratty of Notre Dame, a Pennsylvania-born lad who seemed like the right man to run the team in the 1970's. But Hanratty hadn't really impressed, so Noll still kept an open mind. He also had good reports on Phipps, San Diego State's Dennis Shaw, and Bradshaw.

"I had never seen Terry in person before I went to Miami," Noll recalls, "but the minute I saw him walk onto the practice field I thought to myself, 'He's an athlete.' Then I watched him begin throwing. I was really startled.

I knew from the films that he had a strong arm, but film doesn't measure intensity. He really winged it in there."

Unfortunately, Terry suffered a hamstring pull that day and it slowed him down a bit. It also gave Peterson the final reason to start his own boy, Cappleman. Terry played part of the second and fourth quarters, and ran the team well. When someone asked him if the hamstring bothered him, Terry exploded, "Bull!" he said. "I didn't play more because the coach wanted Cappleman in there. Now I'm going to Mobile for the Senior Bowl and I'm going to beat him (Cappleman) out."

By now, Noll was thinking more and more about drafting one of the quarterbacks, and he hopped a plane to Mobile five days before the Senior Bowl game.

The coaches timed the players in the 40-yard dash. Terry sprinted the distance in 4.7 seconds, very good time for quarterback. But in doing that, he pulled the hamstring muscle again and his coach, Don Shula, offered to let him sit the game out. Terry wouldn't hear of it.

"I went down to Mobile to beat out Cappleman, win the position, start, and have a good game. Nothing was going to stop me."

That's what really impressed Noll. He watched Terry in practice, setting up and throwing despite the injury, responding to top-flight competition like a pro.

In the game itself, Terry started and played very well, winging his passes with authority and hitting his receivers. In the third quarter he was hit hard and suffered two broken ribs. Yet he continued to play. The game ended in a 27-27 tie. Terry had completed 17 of 31 passes for 267 yards and two TDs, and was named the game's Most Valuable Player. Now the Steelers had settled on Bradshaw as the man. Their only remaining question was whether to trade him for established players, or make him their quarterback.

They just looked at Terry as a football player. With offers coming in right up to draft time, the Steelers made their decision. They picked Terry Bradshaw.

"I'm thrilled to death," was Terry's first reaction. "I had a hunch I might go high, maybe first round. But being the number one pick is the most exciting thing that's ever happened to me."

Now Terry had to negotiate his contract with the Steelers. Taking some advice from Roman Gabriel and his dad, Terry decided to do his own negotiating with help from a personal friend, a local attorney from Shreveport. He stayed away from the high-powered agents who had come into vogue about that time.

Slowly, he began to see himself within a much larger scheme of things.

"I was very happy to be chosen by the Steelers," he said. "I wanted to go to a losing team all along. That way, if the team became a winner they'd do it with me. From the first time I went to Pittsburgh and met some of the guys and the coaches, I knew the Steelers were a team in search of a leader. That's what I'm going to be paid for . . . to be a leader."

Before long he had signed his contract, a six-figure package, estimated in the $200,000 to $300,000 range. He was well satisfied. He was also beginning to reap the reward of being an instant "personality."

Not even the instant celebrity treatment could change his basic nature. Still a devout Baptist and already a long-time member of the Fellowship of Christian Athletes, Terry continued doing volunteer church work in the summer, acting as a youth director for underprivileged kids.

"I've always said that I'm a Christian who happened also to be an athlete," he once told a reporter. "Any time I have the chance to speak to kids I tell them that everyone isn't selected to be the same thing in life. Whether it's an athlete, or something else, you've got to accept it for what it is.

"I always figured it this way. It was the Lord who gave me this body and strong arm and if the arm went dead on me tomorrow, it would just be Him taking it back. I believe—and believe strongly—in God, and I don't think it's a cornpone thing."

So Terry was his own man and seemed to know where he was going. When he got to the Steeler camp, it soon became obvious that his main competition would be Terry Hanratty. The other quarterbacks, Dick Shiner and Kent Nix, would soon be on their way to other teams. Hanratty was less than impressive his rookie year of '69. He had trouble handling the big pass rush and hitting his receivers. He connected on just 52 of 126 attempts, a 41.3 average, for 716 yards and eight touchdowns. Thirteen of his passes were picked off. So the battle for the top job would be a wide-open affair between the two Terrys.

By the time the exhibition season rolled around, Coach Noll was alternating his two quarterbacks. Hanratty played the first and third quarter in the opener against the Dolphins, with Bradshaw relieving in the second and fourth. Miami won the game, 16-10, but it was Bradshaw, as usual, who did most of the impressing.

Blond Terry completed nine of 19 passes, with another five dropped by receivers not used to the velocity with which he threw. He engineered Pittsburgh's only touchdown drive.

"I wasn't really pleased with my performance," he said later. "I made a lot of dumb rookie mistakes and didn't do a good job of reading defenses."

Then Terry admitted that something happened in the huddle that he kind of expected. "On the second play of the second series I ran, they all came back yakking and laughing it up. I felt they were testing me, but it made me mad. As a rule I don't like to cuss anyone out, but this time I said, 'Let's cut out the damn fooling around and get down to business.' They were quiet for the rest of the time I played."

Miami coach Don Shula didn't agree with Terry's critical self-analysis. After the game the Dolphin mentor said, "I've been a Bradshaw man all along. He's tough and strong and has a great arm. Plus he's a remarkable athlete."

Chuck Noll agreed. He wanted to take a longer look at his rookie and played him all the way the next week against Minnesota. All Terry did was complete 12 passes and lead his club to a 20-13 victory. He was progressing right on schedule.

The following week the Steelers came into Pittsburgh for their first game in brand-new Three Rivers Stadium. They were facing old rivals, the New York Giants, and Terry once again had the nod as the starting quarterback.

This time he was really hot. Directing the Steeler offense like a 10-year veteran, he quickly got his club on the board with two early touchdowns. The second was a beauty, a 37-yard touchdown strike to rookie Ron Shanklin and the crowd went wild.

When Bradshaw came to the sideline to give way to Hanratty they screamed for his return, and they got him again in the second half, as he continued to lead his club to an easy 21-6 win. Along the way he completed 15 of 23 passes for 244 yards, and he used his ground game very well to keep the young Giant defense off-balance. He was beginning to compile some impressive pro statistics.

"How far can a team go with a rookie quarterback?" Chuck Noll asked himself after the game. Then he answered his own question. "I really don't know. But this is a different kind of rookie."

As for Terry, it was like a dream come true. "The new stadium . . . we won . . . my girl was there. It was all beautiful. I wasn't nervous at all today. I started seeing more things out there, especially my secondary receivers.

I was looking and I was reading, and that's what it's all about."

Terry's girl was Melissa Babish, Miss Teenage America in 1969. They began dating in 1970 and were married in April of 1972.

As the season neared, Terry was brimming with confidence. "They way I feel," he told the press, "there isn't anyone in the world who can move this club like I can. Really, I can just feel it."

The pre-season statistics bore out his prediction. He had truly moved them more effectively than Hanratty. The team had won four straight exhibitions after the loss to Miami, including a convincing win over the rugged Oakland Raiders, and Terry was instrumental in every one of them. He completed 51 percent of his pre-season passes for 663 yards and three scores. His arm and running ability continued to impress people, and his confidence made everyone believe that the Steelers could win. It was a team that had not taken any kind of title in some 38 years and the fans were hungry. They could wait until the opener against Houston rolled around.

Besides Bradshaw, rookie Shanklin and Dave Smith gave the club two fine receivers, while John Fuqua and Preston Pearson were more than adequate runners. Both lines were improving, but many of the young players lacked important experience. Still, many predicted a .500 year or better, which was quite optimistic in view of the 1-13 finish of the year before.

Bradshaw's goals were simple. "I want to be the greatest passer who ever played," he said. "I want to be the best quarterback in the game."

But there were some tough nuts to crack in the Oiler game. Terry would be throwing to three rookie receivers, and they'd be going against a very rough secondary. Terry wanted to strike fast. On the second play of the game he lofted a long pass toward Hubie Bryant. If he connected it would have been a touchdown. But he missed.

After that, everything seemed wrong. Either his passes were dropped by nervous receivers or they wobbled and missed their mark. Perhaps he was nervous, too. Shanklin got free in the second quarter, but the ball slipped off Terry's hand. Instead of a bullet, it was a floater, and the receiver had to stop and wait for it. Another sure touchdown went down the drain.

On the other hand, Houston was doing a nice job. Speedy Jerry Levias caught two TD passes and the Oilers had a 16-0 lead midway in the third period. Bradshaw's passes were still way off the mark, and Noll finally made a decision. He sent Terry Hanratty into the game. The hometown Pittsburgh fans were shocked to silence.

When it ended, Houston had won, 19-7, with Hanratty leading the Steelers to their only score. Bradshaw had had a miserable afternoon, completing just four of 16 for 70 yards. His brilliant exhibition season seemed like a memory from the distant past. Even he couldn't understand what happened.

"I felt so good out there," he said. "Then I did so poorly. I can't figure it out. All those people expected so much. I thought I was loose and relaxed, but nothing seemed to work."

The next week the team traveled to Denver. Terry was back at the helm for a second chance. Surely, it had just been a bad game, nothing more.

Statistically, the Denver game was better, but not the outcome. The Broncos won, 16-13, as Terry completed 13 of 26 passes for 211 yards. But none of his tosses went for scores. He came out of the game only when he was momentarily racked up by tackle Dave Costa—he was "getting his bell rung," as the pros say. But there were still a lot of mistakes.

Against Cleveland the next week Terry had a similar

day. He hit on 13 of 29 for 207 yards, but he had three picked off and didn't throw a score. The Browns won, 15-7. Bradshaw was simply not taking his team into the end zone. He couldn't take it in from the five, the 10, or the 12, and that's losing football.

"I'm having trouble with my passing form," he said. "I'm just not setting up right and there's no zip on the ball. I haven't been throwing the way I did in college."

After four games, the man with the golden arm had completed just 33 passes in 83 attempts for a 39.8 percentage. He hadn't thrown for a single score and had been intercepted five times. In addition, he was dropped for a safety in each of the first three games. His performance on the heels of the fine exhibition season was a complete mystery.

The next week Terry tossed his first TD, a 67-yard bomb to Ron Shanklin and it gave Pittsburgh a 7-3 win over Houston. Then the word came out of the Steeler camp that the quarterback had been fined for missing a squad meeting. He had returned to Louisiana to visit his ailing mother and failed to make it back on time.

Then, two weeks later, the bottom fell out of Terry Bradshaw's season. He had been 12 for 27 for only 138 yards and four intercepts in a 31-14 loss to Oakland. Then, playing against Cincinnati, he couldn't do anything right, hitting just four of 12 for 40 yards. Noll yanked him early and Hanratty came on to lead the club to a 21-10 victory.

After the game, Terry lost his cool for the first time. Talking to reporters well within earshot of Hanratty, Terry said, "I don't want to play second fiddle to Terry Hanratty. I wouldn't mind if it was someone older, someone ready to retire, but I sure won't play behind someone my age. If the Steelers are planning on that, they better trade me."

The pop-off was ill-timed and even more ill-conceived.

Noll was visibly upset and simply retorted by saying that "Terry has a lot of growing up to do, both on and off the field."

Nothing worked well after that. Terry didn't even get into the game against the New York Jets the following week. Hanratty went all the way and the club won, 21-17. From that point on, with the exception of one other game, Hanratty was the starter with Bradshaw pitching relief. According to one story, Bradshaw's frustration grew so great that he went out to his car after one game and cried.

Seasoned observers could sense the team's on-field attitude changing. "The blocking appeared crisper, the holes a little wider when Hanratty ran the team," one said.

There were some incredibly bad days, like a three-for-20 afternoon against Green Bay and a three-for-12 outing against Atlanta. In the finale against Philadelphia, Terry didn't play long enough to throw a single pass.

Terry was a hero just once, in the second game with Cleveland. He completed just four of nine, but they were long ones, going for 197 yards and two TDs. The team won that one, 28-9. Otherwise, all the games were losses, and when it was over the Steeler record was 5-9, and that was after a 4-4 start.

The final statistics were appalling. Terry Bradshaw, the most talked about rookie since Namath, had completed just 83 of 218 passes for 1,410 yards. His passing percentage was an atrocious 38.1. He threw just six TDs, was intercepted 24 times and sacked 25 times. Hanratty didn't do much better with percentages. Yet his experience showed as he threw just eight intercepts and was sacked only three times. He had five TD passes.

If someone wanted to make a direct comparison with rookie Namath, Broadway Joe's 1965 stats read 164 completions in 340 attempts, a percentage of 47.2, with 2,220 yards gained, 18 touchdowns, and just 15 intercepts. It was quite a difference.

Asked about his season, Terry had to be honest. "I wouldn't want another year like it for anything in the world. But on the other hand, I got much of the experience I needed. I created a bad press with my mouth and bad performance with my arm.

"As the season went on I was losing confidence steadily. I just wasn't doing my job. When it was over, I just wanted to get away from Pittsburgh as fast as I could. I wanted to go home, stay away from football so I could relax and get the season out of my mind."

Fortunately, the young mind is capable of bouncing back. By February, Terry reported that he was mentally ready and anxious for the new season to start. "This time I'd have to beat out Hanratty on my own. If I didn't produce on the field, he'd play and well deserve it. I just had to be in the right frame of mind, despite the terrible letdown of my rookie year.

"To be honest, I thought I could do it all in one year, I really did. I didn't realize that in pro football you start from scratch. You have to relearn everything from the very beginning. It's a brand new ballgame all the way."

Once training camp opened at St. Vincent College in Latrobe, Pennsylvania, it was obvious that Terry was out to prove himself once more. His tremendous physical assets once again made him the man Pittsburgh seemed to be depending on. Forgetting the disciplinary incidents of the first year, Coach Noll went back to praising his handsome young signalcaller.

"He can stick the ball in there like nobody else," said Noll.

And John Fuqua, the Steelers top runner, indicated that the rest of the squad had forgotten the uneasiness of the previous season. All they were thinking about was football.

"A lot of things confused Terry last year," said Fuqua. "But now when you stand with him in the huddle at practice you can see there's a difference. He calls the defenses and is seeing more things, like where the linebackers are moving. He didn't notice these things at all last year."

Noll also pointed out an interesting statistic about the club. "Our passing percentage as a team was just 38 percent last year, but our average gain per completion was the best in the league. So our quarterbacks were doing something right. We know we can strike for distance. Now we need greater consistency, especially in short-yardage situations."

In an exhibition game against arch-rival Cincinnati, Terry moved the club well, but still had trouble with the inconsistency. He got the only Steeler touchdown on a short run, but also got his bell rung in the fourth quarter, prompting a couple of Bengal defenders to say that he was running the ball too much. "If he keeps doing that, he'll really get hurt," said tackle Steve Chomyszak.

The Steelers finished the exhibition season with a 3-2 mark, but when the club opened the regular season against Chicago, it looked suspiciously like 1970 all over again. Bradshaw was named the starter after another fine preseason, but somehow he caught a case of the jitters again when it began for real.

He completed just 10 of 24 passes for 129 yards. He failed to throw for a touchdown and had four of his tosses picked off by an alert Chicago secondary. Still, it took two fumble recoveries in the last four minutes for the Bears to push across the scores that gave them a 17-15 victory.

After the game, Noll reaffirmed Bradshaw as his number one quarterback, claiming that Hanratty was strictly a backup performer. He also said that the news media buildup was hurting Terry's game. The only encouraging part of the Bear game was that the Steelers won the battle of statistics.

The next week against Cincinnati they won, 21-10, with Terry connecting on 18 of 30 passes for 249 yards.

He hit Dave Smith with a 16-yard TD toss, then flipped a 13-yarder to Preston Pearson. When Terry came back with a 15-of-24 performance in a win over San Diego, it was beginning to look as if he was finally finding the touch.

He completed 12 of 27 against Cleveland, 20 of 39 versus Kansas City, 21 of 32 against Houston, and 20 of 35 when the Steelers met Baltimore. Bradshaw was much better, yet the club's record was 3-4. There were still a few holes to be filled, especially on defense, and it didn't appear as if the team would do much better than that. Yet some experts saw the potential and began counting the Steelers as one of the clubs with a bright future.

There were some inconsistencies in the second half of the year. In a big win over Cleveland, Terry completed just four of 11 for 70 yards before being replaced by Hanratty. He came back to have a tremendous 25-of-36 day against the Dolphins, throwing for three scores before Miami pulled it out in the final seconds. But he was just six of 17 against Denver and 14 of 31 versus Houston. That prompted his only benching of the season. But he came off the bench to throw fourth-quarter touchdowns to Fuqua and Ron Shanklin in a 21-13 upset of the Bengals.

Coming into their final game, the Steelers were 6-7. They wanted a win, so that they would have a .500 season. But they'd be playing the powerful Los Angeles Rams, and it wouldn't be easy.

In the Cincinnati game, Hanratty fractured a collarbone. Noll had used rookie Bob Leahy before turning to Bradshaw that day. But when Terry pulled it out, he assured himself a start for the finale.

Terry admitted that he had lost some of his confidence in the second half of the 1971 season. Yet he knew where he wanted to go as a quarterback.

"I've got to learn to control the ball better," he said. "That's the first thing. Then I've got to cut down on the interceptions. And, finally, I've got to start coming up with the big play on more occasions. When I sit back and evaluate this season, I'll see how far I've come to attaining these goals. If I feel I've made progress, I'll be satisfied. I certainly wasn't satisfied with my first year."

There was one final disappointment. The Rams were simply too tough for the young Steelers. Los Angeles jumped to a quick 13-0 lead in the first quarter, and Terry had to play catch-up football. He tossed a three-yard TD pass to tight end Larry Brown in the second period, and a two-yarder to Shanklin in the third. But he also threw four more interceptions, and the Rams won, 23-14.

So another year had ended. The Steelers were 6-8, and Terry Bradshaw was still no superstar, though his 1971 season marked a vast improvement over 1970. He had thrown the ball 373 times, completing 203 for 2,259 yards. His passing percentage was up to 54.4. On the other hand, he threw for just 13 touchdowns as compared with 22 interceptions. He was the eighth-ranking passer in the AFC.

Terry gave much of the credit for his improvement to new quarterback coach Babe Parilli. "The man taught me so much," said Bradshaw. "He taught me things about football I didn't even know existed. He made me into a quarterback instead of just a thrower. I think the statistics speak for themselves."

Parilli gave the praise right back. "Joe Namath is a great quarterback," said the Kentucky Babe, who once played behind Broadway Joe. "And Terry Bradshaw is going to be a great quarterback. Joe can't set up to pass any quicker than Terry. And his arm is as good as anyone's, anywhere. All he needs now is more experience.

"At the end of last season he was starting to realize that he could gain as much yardage with a short pass, rather than a long bomb. His receivers are the ones who can cover the ground. But his playcalling improved and he got away from the hit-or-miss tendencies of his rookie year."

The Steelers looked to be a much-improved club in 1972. The defense was quickly evolving into a crack unit. Flanker Frank Lewis, a second-year man from Grambling, and rookie fullback Franco Harris of Penn State, were giving the team a big lift on offense. Kicker Roy Gerela had one of the better toes in the league. This time all the pressure wasn't on Terry.

Pittsburgh had a tough opponent in the opener, the brutal Oakland Raiders, a team whose defense had been chewing up quarterbacks for years. But this time Terry Bradshaw was ready for them.

In the first quarter, Pitt linebacker Henry Davis gave his club a big boost by blocking a punt, grabbing the ball, and carrying it into the end zone. Minutes later, another young linebacker, Jack Ham, intercepted an Oakland pass. Terry moved the club to the Raider 21, then bolted up the middle on a surprise keeper play and blasted through the Oakland secondary all the way to paydirt. It was a 14-0 game.

Oakland rallied for a score, then Bradshaw brought his team into position for two Gerela field goals. Another march produced Terry's second TD as he scored on a three-yard plunge. The score was 27-7. But then the Raiders came back to score 21 fourth-quarter points and take the lead, 28-27. It looked like the old Steelers again.

Only this time Bradshaw kept his cool. With the ball on his own 43, he dropped back, stayed in the pocket, and lofted a long pass in the direction of Ron Shanklin. The fleet receiver grabbed it near the goal line and went in untouched to complete the 57-yard play. The Steelers held on to win it, 34-28. Terry had completed just seven of 17 passes, but he hit when it counted, ran beautifully, and kept control of the game. For his efforts, he was named Associated Press Player of the Week.

Terry was modest, claiming he didn't deserve the honor, but it boosted his confidence nevertheless. He needed it. The next week the club was beaten by Cincinnati, 15-10. There were several questionable calls, however. Terry threw one TD pass to Shanklin that was called back, and connected with another long one that would have had the club knocking on the door. But the officials ruled that Shanklin was out of bounds when he caught it. Later, a Gerela field goal was blocked. The Steeler defense hadn't been bad. Cincinnati got all its points on five field goals by Horst Muhlmann.

Somehow, it wasn't a typical loss, and the club rebounded quickly to defeat St. Louis, 25-19. The next week, Dallas whipped Pittsburgh in another close one, 17-13, and suddenly the season had reached an early turning point. But there was another event that was to greatly alter the course of the year. Strangely enough, it had nothing to do with Terry Bradshaw.

In the Dallas game, fullback Preston Pearson sustained a serious injury, and rookie Franco Harris was installed in his place. The next week Pittsburgh beat Houston, 24-7, as Harris rambled for more than 100 yards. Three more big wins followed, against New England, Buffalo, and Cincinnati. In each game, the 6-2, 230-pound Harris ran wild, going over the century mark and evoking comparisons with the great Jim Brown. He gave the Steelers the big running game they'd always lacked, and helped take even more of the pressure off Terry.

The Steelers were 6-2 and in contention for the Central Division title in the AFC. And Steeler fans, who had focused on Terry for two years, were discovering other heroes—Harris for one. Franco had a black American father and an Italian mother. Suddenly, Italian-American fans of the Steelers formed "Franco's Italian Army," sat together with banners, and rooted for the big running back.

Another group of fans were taken by the sensational soccer-style kicks of Gerela, and they formed a rooting section called "Gerela's Gorillas." Not to be outdone, some Slovak fans rooted for "Dobre Shunka," the "Great Ham," in honor of linebacker Jack Ham who was having an all-pro season. The Steelers had an identity now, and with the pressure off, Terry could just go out and run the football team.

After beating Kansas City, the Steelers were upset by Cleveland, 26-24, to throw the divisional race into a two-team affair. A win over the Vikings seemed almost routine, as all the Steelers looked forward to the rematch with the Browns. The winner would likely take the title.

The game was played in Pittsburgh on December 3, and more than 55,000 fans came out to cheer their beloved team. The Steelers hadn't won in 40 years of NFL competition. Now the whole town was wild.

Cleveland took the opening kickoff. But four plays later Bo Scott fumbled and linebacker Andy Russell recovered it. Bradshaw came on, and moved the team to the 29. Then Gerela booted a perfect 36-yard field goal. Gerela's Gorillas went wild, as did the rest of the fans, and Pittsburgh was on the scoreboard at 3-0.

Harris ran for a touchdown early in the second quarter to make it a 10-0 game. Meanwhile, the Steeler defense was completely blanketing Mike Phipps and the Browns.

It stayed 10-0 into the third quarter. That's when Ham got into the act, intercepting a Phipps pass and running it to the Browns' six. After an exchange of fumbles, Harris scored his second touchdown and it was 17-0. A few minutes later, Terry reminded fans about his throwing arm, winging a 78-yard TD pass to Lewis. Gerela added another pair of field goals, and Pittsburgh won the ballgame, 30-0.

Two weeks later, the Steelers closed with a 24-2 victory over San Diego, and had themselves an 11-3 season, a divisional title, and a trip to the NFL playoffs.

The year's sensational performances by so many of the Steeler players took Terry out of the limelight for the first time in his career. Franco Harris was great all year. He had gained 100 or more yards in six straight games and finished fourth in the AFC with 1,055 yards on just 188 carries. His 5.6 average per carry was among the best in the league. Gerela finished second to the Jets' Bobby Howfield in scoring with 119 points, making good on 28 of 41 field goal attempts.

As for Terry, he had a steady, albeit unspectacular season. But he was still the engineer of the 11-3 mark, and that couldn't be ignored. Statistically, he completed 147 of 308 passes for 1,887 yards and 12 touchdowns. He wasn't throwing as much because of the powerful running attack. His percentage was just 47.7 but he reduced his interceptions to 12, and that had to be a big plus.

With the newly effective zone defenses, many teams were throwing more to their tight ends, and that was a weak point in the Pittsburgh offense. Shanklin was the leading receiver with 38 catches. It wasn't yet an all-pro year for Bradshaw, but it was surely his most consistent since coming up.

"I think I've matured both on and off the field," he told reporters. "My biggest adjustment has been learning to read defenses, but I feel I've made good progress and will continue to make progress."

In the opening round of the playoffs, the Steelers had to face powerful Oakland. They remembered their opening-day 34-28 win against the Raiders, but so did the Raider players. Said fullback Marv Hubbard: "Nobody has beaten us twice in a row. Some teams in our division beat us, but when we played them again, we got even."

The game was played at Pittsburgh on December 23. It

will go down as one of the best and strangest games in NFL annals. The two teams were similarly matched, with strong defenses on both sides. For the first half, it was just that, an epic defensive battle, neither team able to score. It began to look as if neither team would break the ice. Oakland's Daryle Lamonica wasn't throwing well, the Pittsburgh line contained their running game. Bradshaw was doing better, but his receiving corps was depleted by the loss of Lewis to an injury, so the Raider defense was keeping them honest.

Midway through the third period, Terry led a drive downfield that stalled at the 11. Gerela came on and booted an 18-yard field goal. The Steelers were on the scoreboard. In the fourth period, it happened again, this time Gerela hitting from the 29. It was 6-0, with the game entering the final session and the Pittsburgh fans beginning to taste victory.

Then Raider coach John Madden made a move. He installed young Ken Stabler at quarterback. Stabler began moving the team, and with about a minute and a half left, he had his club at the Pittsburgh 30. Stabler faded to pass, saw his receivers covered, and took off. Suddenly, he had a wall of blockers in front of him and he streaked down the sideline toward paydirt. The Steeler crowd couldn't believe it as the young QB ran into the end zone for a score. The kick by ancient George Blanda put the Raiders on top, 7-6, for the first time. There was just a minute and thirteen seconds left.

The kickoff went out of the end zone and the Steelers had it at the 20. Bradshaw had to move the team at least close enough for Gerela to have a shot at a three-pointer.

It was no secret that Terry would have to throw. That he did, dropping back five straight times. Two were broken up by free safety Jack Tatum, and two connected with receivers, bringing the ball to the 40-yard line of

Pitt. There were five seconds left when Terry Bradshaw faded back to throw his final pass.

The original play called for Terry to throw to reserve wide receiver Barry Pearson. But Pearson was covered. Instead, Terry threw over the middle toward halfback John Fuqua. Fuqua was covered by one defender and Tatum rushed up to bat away the ball. It descended into the maze of bodies, then deflected backwards about seven yards. For a split second all action stopped. It looked as if the game was over.

Then there was movement. Franco Harris was streaking toward the Raider goal line with the football. One Oakland defender took up the chase, but it was too late. Harris rambled the remaining 40 or so yards to complete . . . to complete what? For a minute, no one knew what had happened.

Gradually, it became clear. The football had deflected off Tatum's chest. Since Fuqua hadn't touched it, the ball was still in play. Harris, who was actually not involved in the original pattern, suddenly saw the pigskin coming at him. Instinctively, he grabbed it and took off. By the time the startled Raiders recovered, Harris had gone all the way in. The play was legal. The Steelers had won the ballgame, 13-7.

The play was viewed time and again on replay to erase any doubts about its legality. But the Steelers had won. Terry had completed 11 of 25 for 144 yards, but he was helped immensely by the final turnabout, and refused to take any credit for what happened. Now Pittsburgh would meet unbeaten Miami for the AFC crown. There was no time to rest on any laurels.

Once more the Steelers had the home field advantage, and their fans swarmed all over Three Rivers Stadium. Terry was on the field looking no worse for wear and he started the game. Midway through the first period he had his club driving. With the ball at the three, Terry carried around left end. He was hit hard at the goal line and fumbled the ball, but tackle Gerry Mullins fell on it for a Steeler touchdown. It gave Pittsburgh a 7-0 lead, but Terry was shaken up on the play.

Still, Pittsburgh was dominating. Midway through the second period they held Miami again and Larry Seiple dropped back to punt at his own 38-yard line. He took the snap, started his motion—then suddenly took off and ran. The Steelers were caught napping and Seiple carried the ball 50 yards down to the Pittsburgh 12. It was a turning point. Two plays later Earl Morrall passed to Larry Csonka for the score.

On the Steeler side, there was another change. Bradshaw was still woozy from being hit at the goal line and Hanratty was running the team. He couldn't move it. Gerela booted a 14-yard field goal in the third period, but Miami came right back on a Griese-to-Warfield pass for 52 yards. A short run by Jim Kiick made the score 14-10 after three periods.

Steeler fans still believed in miracles. But the Dolphins were now controlling the game. They drove down again and scored, Kiick taking it in for a second time. With the score at 21-10, the Steelers were getting desperate. Chuck Noll put Terry Bradshaw back in the game.

Weakened by his illness and by getting racked up, Terry nevertheless went to work. He just started firing the football. Three completed passes brought it to the Miami 12, and a fourth to Al Young gave Pittsburgh a touchdown. It was 21-17, and it looked as if Bradshaw was hot.

But when the Steelers got the ball again, the magic was gone. The Dolphin defense was laying for Terry and two of his final three passes were picked off and Miami won the ballgame.

Terry had played about half the game and completed five of 10 passes for 80 yards. It was a disappointing finish. Mean Joe Greene, the huge tackle, expressed Pittsburgh's sentiments when he said, "We still think we have the best team. They're good, but small mistakes make the difference."

No one put the rap on Bradshaw. He went as far as he could under adverse circumstances. He had been really racked on the goal line play, and having been sick so close to game time must have hurt. But he was now playing with a good young team, full of exciting talent.

"This is the team of the future, no doubt about it," Terry Bradshaw said during the 1972 season. "And it doesn't matter who's quarterbacking them."

That prophecy was proved false in 1973. It did matter. Terry opened the season with another year's experience under his belt. Like many other quarterbacks in today's game, he was throwing fewer passes and trying to emphasize ball control and running. He fired 23 passes in an opening win over Detroit, then was under the 20-attempt mark in victories over Cleveland, Houston, San Diego, and a loss to Cincinnati.

Wins over the Jets and Bengals followed, giving the Pittsburghers a 6-1 mark. In spite of an uninspiring season by fullback Franco Harris, Pitt was living up to preseason expectations.

There was one problem. In the Bengal game Terry was hurt, a shoulder separation. He'd be out several weeks. With Terry Hanratty and Joe Gilliam running the ballclub, the Steelers managed wins over Washington and Oakland, their defense doing most of the work. Then suddenly things went sour. Denver, Cleveland and Miami whipped them. Terry returned—rusty—for the Miami game. The Steelers lost.

He pulled things together in the final two games, beating Houston and San Francisco. The club was 10-4, same as the Bengals, but settled for the wild-card berth in the playoffs because the Bengals had scored more points in their two meetings.

The playoff games turned into a rout. Oakland was coming on and whipped Pittsburgh, 33-15. The Pitt defense had been hampered by injuries all year and operating at less than full speed.

Terry threw just 180 passes in 1973, completing 89 for 1,183 yards and 10 TDs. He was intercepted 15 times. But it was an incomplete year. The shoulder injury and playoff loss made it that way. There was little doubt that the Steelers had the potential to be great. But the question remained: Would Terry Bradshaw be the quarterback who would lead them to that ultimate victory?

To many, Terry was no longer the man with the Golden Arm. In fact, for one reason or another, Terry was becoming the victim of a cruel and tormenting crusade. It was being said in many circles that he lacked certain intellectual abilities that go along with being a top-flight quarterback. In other words, people were saying that Terry Bradshaw was dumb!

The charge hurt Terry badly. All kinds of skeletons were being dug out of the closets. For instance, when the Steelers drafted Terry they were a 1-13 team with poor prospects. Meaning to comment that he was glad he was going to a team that he could help build into a winner, Terry managed a poor selection of words. He said, "I always wanted to go with a loser." Things like that, perhaps meaningless at the time, we're now being pointed out as proof of Terry's faults. And it wasn't fair. Plus some of the Steeler fans were really beginning to work him over.

The booing was one thing. All quarterbacks experience that at one time or another. But the day of Terry's shoulder separation in 1973, he was sitting in his car at a gas station, in pain, his arm in a sling, when several young fans approached.

"I thought they were going to say something like,

'Hang in there,'" relates Terry, "but instead they made an obscene gesture and called me a vile name. I guess I was naive, but I really didn't know what life was all about when I came to this town."

Now Terry was in the unenviable position of having to defend his own intellect.

"I know I'm not dumb. I've got a good football mind," he said. "I think about 90 percent of the touchdown passes I threw last year came on audibles. I can read defenses as well as Namath, Griese, or anyone. There's no set I don't recognize. I am not dumb."

It was a shame that things had to come to that. Terry also knew he'd have to prove himself on the field. And to make matters worse, his marriage was going sour and coming to an end. Things were pretty bad for him when the 1974 preseason got underway.

Terry was unsure in the exhibitions, his timing was off. Sometimes it seemed as if his mind was elsewhere. At the same time, former third-string QB Joe Gilliam was coming off the bench to fire one TD pass after another. Gilliam was a black quarterback, and since no black had ever been a regular signalcaller in the NFL, he began getting a wealth of publicity. By the time the pre-season came to an end, Coach Noll announced that Gilliam had won the Steeler quarterbacking job. And Bradshaw's critics had their chance to gloat. As for Terry, he was crushed.

"It was the lowest point of my career," he admits freely. "I just couldn't understand why it was happening. I couldn't take anything away from Gilliam. He had an outstanding exhibition season and was producing. He deserved to play.

"But my own idea was that a quarterback shouldn't lose his job in the exhibition season. I use the exhibition games to prepare myself for the season. I'm not out to set any records in those games. But Chuck Noll had to make a decision and he did. I thought then that I'd be traded. I knew I couldn't stand sitting on the bench for an entire season while someone else played."

Gilliam started the first six games of the year, giving the Steelers a 4-1-1 record and the conference lead. But as the season wore on, people were beginning to say that Gilliam was pass-happy, he threw too much, the interceptions were mounting and the team hadn't played the tough opposition yet. Plus Joe seemed to be losing the magic that produced a brace of TDs in the preseason in the first few games. Critics said that the Steeler defense was the reason the club was winning.

Then, before the seventh game against tough Atlanta, Noll suddenly told Terry Bradshaw that he'd be starting. The news shocked both Bradshaw and Gilliam, but Terry responded with a winning effort. He completed just nine of 21 passes, but the club got a 24-14 victory.

"I felt strange out there," said Terry. "My timing was off and I mixed up a couple of handoffs. I could have done better."

Now the question was, who would be the Steeler QB? No one seemed to know. Terry started three straight games. Then, for some reason, Coach Noll gave the third quarterback, Terry Hanratty, a start. But after that, he went back to Bradshaw and the youngster responded with a big game against New Orleans, completing more than half his passes, including two for touchdowns, and running for 99 yards on nine attempts, as Pittsburgh won, 28-7. That seemed to do it. Even the fans sensed the handwriting on the wall. In a local poll, 41 percent of them wanted Bradshaw as the Pittsburgh quarterback. It seemed as if Terry had won the job back.

Terry started the remaining three games and brought the club home with a divisional title and a 10-3-1 record. His stats were unimposing: just 67 completions in 148 tries for a 45.3 percentage. He threw for seven scores and had eight intercepted. But he was calling a good basic game, utilizing his outstanding runners, Franco Harris (who gained 1,006 yards) and Rocky Bleier (a rugged blocker), to control the ball. Plus he was hitting on the big plays.

In addition, the Pitt defense had become the most awesome in the league, led by Mean Joe Greene and a devastating front four. So the Steelers were in the playoffs and according to most had a great shot at the Super Bowl.

In the first playoff game, the Steelers had to face O.J. Simpson and the Buffalo Bills. Terry was really looking forward to that one.

"Sure, I'm looking forward to the game," he said. "The big thing is that my confidence is coming back. Any quarterback on the bench for six weeks has to have a lot of confidence destroyed. But I feel I'm contributing to the offense now and can contribute a lot more."

He was right. Against the Bills, Terry had a great day, hitting on 12 of 19 passes and running for 48 clutch yards. He led the Steelers to a 32-14 rout and into the AFC title game against Oakland.

This one was tougher. The Raiders were big and strong, and took a 10-3 lead into the third quarter on their home field. But Terry stayed cool. He led his club on a long drive that resulted in the tying touchdown, then took charge as the Steelers won big and going away, 24-13. Now it was on to the Super Bowl and a date with the Minnesota Vikings and their great quarterback, Fran Tarkenton. And by now, Terry was oozing confidence.

"I don't think Fran is any better than I am," he said. "I've played in my share of big games. Heck, the last five games have been big and I've been playing well in the ones that have counted."

His past reputation notwithstanding, Terry played extremely well under pressure. He called a cool game. Once he saw how well his running game was working, he stuck with it, allowing Franco Harris to set a Super Bowl rushing record of 158 yards as the club gained 249 yards on the ground, another record. He passed only when he had to, completing nine of 14 for 96 yards, as the Steelers become World Champions with a 16-6 win. For Terry, it was the happiest day of his life.

"What I was doing out there today was just what I'm capable of doing," he said, "what I've taken the time and patience to learn how to do. This thing about my having no brains has been passed down for years. I have a label and I'm just going to have to live with it. But I've already faced a lot of adversity, like the criticisms and being benched, and I withstood it. I've looked at both sides, being a hero and a bum, and I think I can handle this very well. But it was a complete team effort. The entire club was great."

So things finally began falling into place for Terry. After the season he was named Louisiana's Outstanding Professional Athlete. It might seem a minor award, but it made him feel very good. Now he just wanted to produce consistent winning football over an entire season.

A relaxed Terry looked forward to 1975. He had a great preseason, completing nearly 60 percent of his passes. With a team like the Steelers, it was easy. Plus the quarterback job was his now, and unless he blew it, his to keep. Pretty soon he was beginning to produce outstanding efforts under pressure.

Against Houston he took the Steelers on a 78-yard drive in the closing minutes, accounting for 76 of those yards himself, either by passing or running, to give the club a victory.

"Part of being a championship team is being tough in the fourth period," said Coach Noll. "That's when games are decided. And this one was a good example. It was also one of the better games Terry has played."

That wasn't all. Against tough Cincinnati Terry completed 13 of 24 with two TDs, plus scored one running as Pitt won, 30-24. Against the Chiefs, he was 16 of 24 in a 28-3 rout. Franco Harris was on his way to another 1,000 yard year, and the defense continued to be great. In addition, wide receiver Lynn Swann was beginning to show he was as spectacular as any deep threat in the league.

More good things were happening to Terry. He had become engaged to ice skating star Jo Jo Starbuck, and the two planned to marry after the season.

When the season ended, the Steelers were atop their division with a 12-2 mark and headed for the playoffs once again. And Terry finally had that big year everyone was waiting for. He was fifth in the entire NFL in passing, with 165 completions in 286 tries for a 57.7 percentage, 2,055 yards, and 18 TDs. This time he had just nine passes intercepted. He also ran for an additional 210 yards.

Then, in the playoffs, he proved his mettle once again. Despite a painful leg injury that forced him from the game in the second quarter, Terry came back after halftime to lead the Steelers to a 28-10 win over Baltimore. The score was just 7-7 when he was hurt, so Terry knew he had to return.

"I couldn't feel it at all in the second half," he said, "so I let the running game go."

Harris came through with 153 yards, but Terry also completed eight of 13 passes, hitting when he had to, as the Steelers dominated the second half.

Though he couldn't run well, Terry was at the helm as the Steelers faced the Raiders again for the AFC crown. It wasn't an easy game, but the all-around talents of the Pittsburgh team prevailed and the Steelers won, 16-10. Now it was on to the Super Bowl once again, with the opponent the Dallas Cowboys.

Terry was ready for this one. Though Dallas led, 10-7,

at halftime, Terry didn't panic. A safety made it a 10-9 game, then Terry drove his club into Dallas territory twice, allowing Roy Gerela to boot a pair of field goals that made it 15-10. It was still anyone's game when Pitt took control again late in the game. The ball was on their own 36. It was a third and five play with three minutes left. Everyone thought Terry would go for the first down and then try to eat up the clock.

But he fooled them. Showing the guts and confidence that the great ones are made of, he dropped back and lofted a pass deep downfield. On the receiving end was the dynamic Lynn Swann, making a great catch and running into the end zone for a 64-yard TD. Terry didn't even see the play. He waited until the last second to throw, and just as he released the ball he was knocked down hard by the charging Dallas linemen. A dizzy Bradshaw was helped to the sidelines, but his brilliant call was the big one, for Dallas scored again to make it 21-17. That's the way it ended and Pittsburgh had won its second straight Super Bowl.

Terry was nine of 19 in the final game, good for a big 209 yards and two scores. Swann was the MVP for two great catches, but it was Terry who had done the throwing.

Now Terry wanted to continue winning. He was in an enviable position, quarterbacking perhaps the most powerful team in all of pro football. As the 1976 season began, the Steelers' goal was to become the first club to take three straight Super Bowls.

Then something happened. The club was making mistakes, especially the defense, which had been so magnificent. They lost their opener, then won, but then dropped three straight. After five games, the mighty Steelers had a 1-4 record.

There were team meetings, changes in strategy, chewing outs from Coach Noll and several key players. Finally the team began to win. But after a couple of victories Terry injured his neck and wrist. He was on the shelf, and the club turned to a rookie QB, Mike Kruczek, to lead the team.

But by this time the club was in high gear. Franco Harris and Rocky Bleier were once again eating up yards behind the fine offensive line, and the defense, which had made so many mistakes in the first five games, once again played like the league's best.

With Kruczek at the helm, the team continued to win. In fact, they won all six games in which the rookie started. The overall winning streak had reached eight when Terry was finally ready to return. The club was 9-4. Still they had to win their final game to make the playoffs. That would tie them with the Cincinnati Bengals with 10-4 marks, but Pitt would be in the playoffs because they had whipped the Bengals twice earlier in the year.

Terry took it easy the first time back, using his runners and relying on his defense. But he looked confident as the club won its game. They had done it, nine straight wins and another shot at the Super Bowl.

As for Terry, he now said he was ready for the playoffs. The layoff and early-season team slump didn't give him much in the way of stats. He completing just 92 of 192 passes for a 47.9 percentage and 1,177 yards. He had 10 TD passes and nine intercepts. But he was still the starting QB against a very tough Baltimore team, which had its own rifle-armed quarterback in Bert Jones. It wouldn't be easy.

But the Steelers were ready. Early in the game Terry found that his runners could slash through the Baltimore defense. He found it out, however, after he had hit flanker Frank Lewis on a 76-yard TD bomb, which came on just the third play of the game.

Then he started running. Even with halfback Rocky Bleier forced out with a bruised toe, the Steeler backs continued to ramble. Fullback Harris had more than 100 yards in the first half alone. But in the third period he, too, left the game with bruised ribs.

But Terry was looking very healthy. In the second period he went to work again and whipped a 29-yard scoring pass to Lynn Swann. And in the final period he hit Swann from 11 yards out for a third score.

The Steelers had really done the job. They came away with a 40-14 victory, with Terry completing 14 of 18 for 264 yards and three scores. It was his best game of the year and couldn't have come at a better time. After the game, however, he had mixed emotions.

"Sure, I felt good out there today," he said, "and I'm certainly happy with the way things turned out. But we've got a tough one with Oakland coming up and I'm kind of afraid to look at that medical report."

He had good reason. Both Bleier and Harris were banged up pretty bad and immediately called "doubtful" for the AFC title game. You can't lose two 1,000-yard runners and not feel it. In addition, ace placekicker Roy Gerela had a groin pull and could not kick with his usual effectiveness. The Raiders, meanwhile, were sky high, looking for revenge against the team that had beaten them in the last two AFC title games.

It didn't go well right from the start. How could it with both Harris and Bleier out? Their injuries were more serious than first thought. Both were out of the game. Terry had to throw and the Raiders were ready.

An Errol Mann field goal gave Oakland a 3-0 lead. Then the Raiders scored again on a short run by Clarence Davis. The Steelers came back to make it 10-7, but two Ken Stabler TD tosses put the game on ice. It ended with the Raiders winning, 24-7, and going on to the Super Bowl. Steeler domination was over.

After the game Terry talked about having to throw so much at the outset.

"I don't like that kind of offense," he said. "I like Rocky and Franco. What could we do? The coaches tried to put something together that they believed in. We had to try it, but it just didn't work. But give the Raiders credit. They beat us. They beat the best. So now they're the best."

Terry was 14 for 35 for 176 yards in the big game, knowing how the Raiders were waiting for him. There will always be people who will wonder how the game would have ended if the Steelers had their great runners.

But Terry Bradshaw didn't complain. It had been a hard season for him, too. The early losses, the injuries, the missed games. He showed he still had it in the victory over Baltimore. He's still the leader of a powerful team. They can come all the way back. And most of the criticism has stopped. Terry is respected now, and that took a while. So he can look forward to the next season and seasons after that. The rifle arm is still there, and the man behind it will always be ready.

He knows now that an NFL quarterback must prove himself over and over again. It may not be the greatest way to earn a living, but Terry Bradshaw wouldn't have it any other way.

# ★ ROGER STAUBACH ★

★ It seems that the miracles will never end for Roger Staubach. The fancy-stepping, hard-throwing quarterback of the Dallas Cowboys is indeed a football magician, who is capable of putting on a magic show of his own every time he takes to the gridiron.

And he's been doing it for a long time. There's not a single fan of college football who doesn't remember Roger's storied career at the United States Naval Academy in the mid-1960's. He was the most exciting player in the country then, exibiting a dash and daring that drove his opponents to distraction.

After his college career ended, Roger had a four-year service obligation, which he unhesitatingly fulfilled. Then he decided to try to play pro ball. Just making the team after such a long layoff would be a miracle. But Roger the Dodger not only made the Dallas Cowboys, two years later he was leading them to a Super Bowl triumph and was being hailed as pro football's new premier quarterback.

But the miracles weren't over. Injuries and a bad season dogged him for two years, then he went to work again. In 1975 he led a Dallas team that was supposed to be in the throes of rebuilding all the way to the pinnacle of the football world—the Super Bowl. There were many other contributing factors, of course, but still the main man in Dallas was Roger Staubach, on the brink of leading his team to yet another miracle season. As the Super Bowl game with the defending champion Pittsburgh Steelers approached, many fans, with the help of the media, relived highlights of the Staubach career. They were quickly reminded that it was a miracle in itself that Roger ever played for the Cowboys in the first place.

When the 1964 professional football draft rolled around, all the teams in both the National and American Leagues began looking over the crop of collegians available to them. General managers met with their coaching staffs, while scouts telephoned in reports from every corner of the land. The most common question asked about a player was: "Where can he fit into our immediate plans?"

Fortunately, Tex Schramm and the rest of his Dallas Cowboy organization had more foresight than that. Sure, they wanted to strengthen their team. The Cowboys had been formed in 1960 and had just completed a 4-10 season. They needed help.

And they drafted for it. Then came the 10th round. Schramm surprised everyone. He made his choice and it was announced at NFL headquarters.

*"The Cowboys pick Roger Staubach, quarterback, Navy."*

*Roger Staubach?* The Cowboys must be crazy! First of all, Staubach was only a junior. He'd be playing for the Midshipmen again next season. But he had gone to prep school for an extra year and since his original class was graduating, he was eligible for the draft as a future.

But what a long future! Besides staying at the Naval Academy for another year, Roger Staubach had a four-year commitment to the service. And anyone who knew Roger Staubach knew he didn't back down on his commitments. Thus, in early 1964, the Cowboys had drafted a quarterback who wouldn't be available to play for them until the fall of 1969. That's a long wait for any man, and it is a proven fact that few athletes can approach their old form after a layoff of four years.

Why, then, did the Cowboys do it?

"Our philosophy," explained general manager Schramm, "in the latter rounds of the draft is to take a gamble, a gamble on greatness. We just hoped that someday Roger would be able to play football for the Cowboys. Of course, there was a chance he wouldn't be commissioned, but we knew we'd likely have to wait five years. We felt strongly that Roger Staubach was a man worth waiting for."

Looking at Staubach's 1963 season at the Naval Academy, it becomes crystal clear why the Cowboys drafted him. As a junior, Roger the Dodger set the college football world on fire. He was the winner of both the Heisman Trophy and the Maxwell Award, the two top prizes given to the best college player in the land. He was everybody's All-America, and he led his team to a 9-1 record and a New Year's Day game with Texas in the Cotton Bowl. His coach, Wayne Hardin, called him simply "the greatest football player I've ever seen."

His individual record was equally phenomenal. Roger completed 107 of 161 passes in that 1963 season, for a completion percentage of 66.4, and 1,474 yards. In addition, he rushed for 418 yards, and led his team to a season-ending rout of Army.

He was the complete quarterback, a pinpoint passer, a scrambler who knew no equal, and a devastating runner, as elusive as he was strong. He controlled a football game like no quarterback Navy had ever seen. In fact, his 1963 season is generally regarded as one of the greatest ever by a college football player anywhere. The way he played, a pro team would probably have waited ten years to get him.

The Middies had a tough schedule in 1963. Coach Hardin took his team up against the likes of Michigan, S.M.U., Pittsburgh, Notre Dame, Duke, and Army. None of that fazed the mighty Staubach. Roger the Dodger was the same elusive personage against them all. Maybe they should have called him the magician, or the invisible man. At least, that's how he must have seemed to the frustrated defensive players who had to chase him all year.

"One thing I learned about Roger," said coach Hardin, "was to let him have his head when he was on the field. When he started to break a pattern, I couldn't tear my hair. He had such great ability, and was such a winner, that I just had to believe that what he was doing would come out all right in the end."

It usually did. Jolly Roger, as he was also called, was never reluctant to go off on a trip of his own. He'd often run to one side of the field, then the other, sidestepping attempted tackles, zigzagging his way past frenzied defenders, spinning, dancing, jumping, twisting, faking. And the chase was usually in vain. It was a game in which the hunted outwitted the hunters. He might scramble for 30 seconds or more, then finally spot an open man, crank his arm, and rifle the ball to paydirt, while his impatient pursuers gasped for breath.

He had a style all his own, a style they said wasn't suited to pro ball, where the pocket passer still reigned supreme. But Roger Staubach was a determined, dedicated young man. And he was a leader, an innovator, a winner. Tex Schramm and the Cowboys saw all these things. They were willing to wait. Sooner or later, they felt, the Jolly Roger would land for good. And Dallas would be the better for it.

The Dodger made his debut in a Cincinnati hospital on February 5, 1942, the only son of Robert and Elizabeth Staubach, both fine, upstanding members of their community. From the first, they taught their son the same values by which they lived their own lives, and young Roger quickly became deeply religious, honest, devoted, and dedicated to whatever enterprise he undertook.

And it didn't take him long to undertake an interest in sports. He started playing football, basketball, and baseball in the CYO leagues in Cincinnati and soon was exhibiting outstanding ability in all three. He went to St. John Evangelist Elementary School and was a good student, but his parents admitted that he always had one eye on the playground. And when he got out there, he'd play ball from morning to night, whichever sport was in season. They were all fine with him.

When he was seven, he began playing baseball on knothole teams which were co-managed by his father.

"Roger could do anything even then," his father says proudly. "We put him wherever we needed a player on that particular day. I remember one time we had to have a catcher. Roger had never played there before, but he stepped in and did a fine job."

One thing that didn't make the grade with young Roger was music lessons. His mother wanted him to play the piano, so they hired a teacher to work with him.

"The boys drove the teacher crazy," Mrs. Staubach recalls. "They'd be out on the porch making all kinds of noise and waiting for Roger to finish. He couldn't wait to get outside either, so we finally called the whole thing off."

As a seventh grader at St. Paul, Roger began playing football. He could already carry the ball so they put him at halfback. He stayed at that position for two years, then entered Purcell High School, where he was moved to end his freshman year. The next season the coach made Roger his quarterback, and the change produced a strange reaction from the young Staubach.

"He came home and cried," says Mr. Staubach. "He really didn't like the idea. He enjoyed running with the ball even then and the Purcell coach didn't like his quarterbacks to run."

Roger really didn't have to worry, because the next season he was switched again, this time to defensive halfback. The coach liked his seniors to have the fun and glory of running the offense, while the juniors did the dirty work on defense. But by then Roger had taken a liking to being the quarterback and he was looking forward to returning to that position as a senior.

Return he did. Before long, it became obvious that Purcell High had a real superstar. Up to that time, Purcell signal-callers rarely ran with the ball. They would hand off, pitch out, or pass. Roger changed all that.

"Roger just ran around back there," one of his teammates said. "Five or six guys from the other team would be chasing him and no one could catch him. The fans went wild and Roger usually turned the play into a big gain."

Purcell High became a big winner, and in their traditional game with arch rival Elder High, Roger really set things on fire. With the defense looking for a pass, the lanky quarterback began scrambling. Then he was past the line of scrimmage and streaking for the sideline. Sidestepping and outmaneuvering several would-be tacklers, Roger streamed downfield on a 60-yard touchdown romp. It won the game and really put young Mr. Staubach on display as a quarterback with a future.

College offers began pouring in. Roger had a choice, of course. Wanting a good football school and still inclined to continue his Catholic education, he looked to Notre

Dame as the only place for him. But the Irish were hesitant, and seemed reluctant to make any concrete offers. In fact, they discussed basketball with him, rather than football.

Other schools were more persistent. Woody Hayes, the coach at Ohio State, figured Roger would fit right in with his ground-oriented attack and made a determined, personal effort to land him.

"Mr. Hayes must have spent a fortune in phone calls," Mrs. Staubach said. "And everything he did was direct, not through an assistant. He spoke with Roger, visited him, and really showed a personal interest."

Purdue was also high on the list. Roger even went as far as to make a tentative acceptance there, but it was never anything concrete. Young Staubach did well academically and was also president of the student council at Purcell, so he was looking for more than a place to play football. That's where the Naval Academy came in.

Richard Kleinfeldt, a prominent Cincinnati resident whose son had played football for Navy, was an ardent supporter of the Academy. He spoke to Roger about attending and then personally took him on a tour of the facilities.

"I think when Roger saw the Academy, he was convinced," Kleinfeldt said. "He realized that it was a place where he could play top-flight football, yet still get his education. And at the same time he could be serving his country. He felt very strongly about doing more in life than just playing ball."

So Roger made his commitment. But he had one more game as a high schooler. It was the annual North-South game featuring all the best seniors in the Cincinnati area.

"He ran wild," says Navy coach Wayne Hardin. "He was by far the best player on the field, on offense and defense, and these were kids from the whole of Cincinnati. I was overjoyed to see it. We were going to get quite a football player, someone I knew could turn our entire program around."

It didn't take long for the Jolly Roger to work his magic at the Academy. Taking charge of the plebe (freshman) team from the start, Staubach led the junior Middies to a fine 8-1 season, and served notice that Coach Hardin had some great talent on the horizon. Roger passed and ran defenses crazy, and it wasn't long before the Academy's Sports Information Director, Budd Thalman, tagged the young star Roger the Dodger.

His sophomore year was one of great expectations, for both Roger and the team. But aside from football, he was finding life at Annapolis much to his liking.

Always devoutly religious, Roger continued to attend Mass daily, even though it meant getting up at 5:45 A.M. every day. Back at 6:30, making his bed and "squaring off" his room, he got set for a full day of activities that didn't end until midnight or thereabout, when he usually fell asleep over a book. He also had a girl, Marianne Hobler, a nurse in Cincinnati whom Roger had known since the first grade. The two planned to marry someday, but he knew that they couldn't be serious about it until he graduated from the Academy. So Roger and Marianne were "engaged to be engaged" for four years. But even that step took a great degree of soul searching on Roger's part. He views every phase of life with the utmost concern.

Fortunately for the Academy, his sense of values included playing the best brand of football he could. As soon as he came out for the varsity, his sophomore year, Coach Hardin knew he had a winner.

"Quarterbacks have to be leaders," the coach said. "They have to show that quality both on and off the field. Roger Staubach is a high class gentleman with the right ideas and morals. He's a born leader."

There was just one problem, something Hardin had to

work out in his own mind. "We had a senior quarterback the year Roger was a sophomore," Hardin recalls. "His name was Ron Klemick and he was a good ballplayer. In fact, the season before, he was instrumental in taking a mediocre team to a fine 7-3 record. He had been outstanding. He threw well and also was a good leader.

"Now I knew Roger was ready. He could step in and just take over. But I wouldn't just kick Klemick in the behind and tell him to sit down. It wasn't right. I told Roger this and told him he'd have to earn the starting position. He said that was fine with him, so we started the season with Klemick at quarterback and Staubach on the bench."

Roger played only four minutes of Navy's 1962 opener against Penn State. It must have been frustrating, because the Nittany Lions buried the Middies, 41-7. The next week, Staubach didn't get in at all, as Klemick led his team past a mediocre William and Mary club, 20-16. Then Minnesota got hold of Navy and won easily, 21-0, with Roger seeing just two minutes of action. Klemick wasn't doing the job and the handwriting was on the wall.

Minutes before the opening kickoff in the Cornell game the following week, coach Hardin made an abrupt decision.

"Roger, warm up. You're starting today," he said.

The Jolly Roger put on his helmet, peeled off his jacket to reveal the number 12 on the back of his jersey, and started throwing the football. A new era in Navy football was about to begin.

With Staubach in the lineup, the Middies jumped to life. Roger quickly added a crispness to the attack that had been missing thus far. He handed the ball to his backs just as they burst past him into the holes. When he went to pass, he dropped back quickly, spotted his receiver, and drilled the ball home. When a play was broken . . . well . . . that's when he really went to work, showing the scramble-stuff that would drive opponents crazy.

Every time Roger took off on one of his journeys, the Cornell players pursued in vain. The elusive number 12 wiggled his shoulders and performed magic with his feet. Eight times he took off overland in that first game, and he picked up 89 yards. His passing was even more impeccable, as he completed nine of 11 for 99 yards and an .818 percentage. He easily led the Midshipmen past their outgunned opponents, 41-0.

"Roger was just super," Hardin said. "He was even better than we thought he'd be. There was no containing him, no way at all. I think Klemick understood. We had a superplayer who was going to improve with each passing week. He couldn't be kept on the bench any longer."

The Jolly Roger continued his rampage, leading the Middies past Boston College and Pittsburgh. In the later game he was perfect, completing eight out of eight passes for a fantastic 192 yards and a touchdown. That's an average of 24 yards gained per pass. Amazing.

Then Navy hit a dry spell. Hardin just didn't have enough depth or experience, and Staubach couldn't do it alone against the power teams. First Notre Dame toppled the Middies, 20-12; then Syracuse did a real job, 34-6, and Southern Cal completed the trio of losses, getting by, 13-6. This was a close one. The Trojans were ranked among the top teams in the country, but Roger gave them fits. He was 11 for 17 passing, and scrambled for 113 yards and a touchdown. The game put the Middies back on the beam and got them ready to meet Army in the season's finale.

There's no way anyone can predict the outcome of an Army-Navy game. The rivalry goes way back to 1890 and when the two teams meet, it's no holds barred. So anxious are both service academies to win the annual clash that coaches are sometimes the first casualties of battle.

Coming into the 1962 game, Navy had beaten Army three straight times. Exit Army coach Dale Hall, despite a good overall record. Enter Paul Dietzel, a young, dynamic coach from Louisiana State with no prior service connections. But Dietzel had built a football power at LSU and had introduced three-platoon football to the land. He had a White Team, his regulars who played both ways for about half the game. Then there was the Go Team, offensive specialists, and the famed Chinese Bandits, his defensive platoon. This way, he used almost all his players and each unit had a pride and a drive all its own.

Army arrived at Philadelphia's Municipal Stadium on December 1, with a 6-3 record, a mark that included wins over Penn State and Syracuse, two teams that had beaten the Middies badly. Navy, on the other hand, was just 4-5, and needed the game for a break-even year. But records mean nothing when these two teams meet.

With President John Kennedy among the 98,616 spectators, Navy drew first blood when an Army punt attempt resulted in a bad pass from center and a safety. The Cadets then drove into Navy territory, only to miss a field goal try from the 27. That's when Staubach went to work.

He passed 39 yards to Ed Merino, then tossed a five-yarder to Bob Teall. He let his backs carry deeper into Army land, then scrambled for eight more himself. With the ball on the Army 12, Jolly Roger dropped back and calmly hit Neil Henderson with a 12-yard scoring pass. The touchdown, coupled with the earlier safety, gave the Middies an 8-0 lead.

The next time Navy got the ball, Staubach struck again. Chinese Bandits notwithstanding, he passed 16 yards to end Jim Campbell. Another quick toss to Dave Sjuggerud found the mark for ten more. Then the backs took over, running the ball to the Army 20. Staubach took the ensuing snap and rolled out to his right. When he saw his receivers covered, he began slithering past Army tacklers like a snake. He sidestepped one, spun off another, faked a third right onto his back, and when he crossed the goal line there were still no hands on him. It was a brilliant run and the extra point gave Navy a 15-0 lead.

Army came back to make it 15-6, but Roger the Dodger wasn't through yet. Early in the third quarter, he eluded two onrushing linemen and coolly tossed a 65-yard scoring strike to fullback Nick Markoff, who was all alone when he caught the ball on the Navy 45 and ran the rest of the way home. It was a great call by Roger, who isolated his back in the middle and hit him with a bullet. The kick made it 22-6, in favor of Navy.

In the final session, Roger led another long drive, firing a 48-yard strike to Campbell, and hitting on two short pitches to halfback Johnny Sai before taking it in himself from the two. Navy led, 28-6, and for all purposes, the game was over right there. The final was 34-14, and the Middies sent the cadets back to West Point in defeat.

As for Roger, he completed an amazing 11 of 13 passes for 188 yards and two touchdowns. He was also Navy's leading rusher with 24 yards on 14 carries, and scored two more touchdowns via the ground. It was a scintillating performance. Roger had finally made believers out of them all.

Staubach didn't have much to say after the game. But when a reporter asked him what happened to the Chinese Bandits, he answered with his usual quiet honesty. "I really can't say it made any difference. I didn't know when the Bandits were in the game and when they weren't."

It was a cinch that Staubach was in the game, though, and with the same basic team returning, the Midshipmen anxiously awaited the start of the 1963 season.

But even before it started, the 6-2, 195-pound signal-caller was the talk of the land. He hadn't made any major All-American teams as a sophomore because his season didn't start until the fourth game, but everyone was predicting big things for him in '63.

Roger's statistics from 1962 served notice. He had completed 67 of 98 passes for 966 yards and a completion percentage of .684. Seven tosses went for touchdowns, and he scored seven more times on the ground, having annexed 265 yards on 85 carries.

He started the next season right where he left off, completing 17 of 22 passes in a 51-7 rout of West Virginia. The next week he was 12 of 17 for 206 yards, and he added another 91 running in a 28-0 blanking of William and Mary. Then Roger led the Middies into their first tough one of the year against Michigan.

It was a hard-fought game from start to finish, and when it ended, the passing of Roger Staubach had taken its toll. The Jolly Roger riddled the Wolverine defense for 14 completions in 16 tries for 237 yards and two scores. He also ran the ball 18 times, gaining 70 yards in a one-man show that had the football world talking once more. P.S.: Navy won, 26-13.

Everyone looked to Annapolis. That's where the action was. That's where Roger Staubach was calling the plays.

Even his coach couldn't believe what was happening. "I've just got to realize that this guy is something special," Hardin confessed. "In the Michigan game they're leading us by a touchdown with less than a minute remaining in the first half. The ball's close to midfield and he calls two straight running plays. I wondered what was going on. The next thing I know he's got the ball up in the air and we've got a touchdown." (Staubach had thrown a 43-yard touchdown pass.)

"Then in the second half we drive to their 18. I watch him roll to the left, then back to the right. Then he's all over the place. Suddenly he's rolling past me and I'm standing on the 50. I was ready to have a nervous breakdown. Then he gets hit and he's parallel to the ground. I figure it's all over. Suddenly he flicks his arm and tosses a pass to Donnelly, who runs it back upfield and we get a one-yard gain. I couldn't believe it."

But the party ended the following week. Navy traveled to the Cotton Bowl in Dallas to meet Southern Methodist University. It was one of the roughest college games ever played, and Roger the Dodger had to pull out every stop just to survive. And he still found time to be magnificent.

Early in the first quarter, a big SMU tackle cracked into Staubach from the blind side. It was one of the few times he didn't see an onrushing lineman. Roger went to the sidelines, holding his left shoulder. The official diagnosis was a stretched nerve, but the Dodger shook off the pain, and returned to bull his way through the center of the Mustang line for a score.

SMU scored two touchdowns on the ground, but Roger came right back to set up a score with a nifty scramble inside the ten. He threw for a two-point conversion and had the Middies back on top, 18-13.

When the second half started, SMU again began gang-tackling the Navy quarterback. It was as if they were going after the bad shoulder, trying to put him out of the game.

"It's the only time I ever saw him angry," Hardin said. "He felt they were taking cheap shots. They hurt his shoulder, bloodied his face, and scratched at him every time his helmet came off. But he never complained."

Ignoring the pain in his left shoulder, Staubach drove his team into SMU territory again, this time tossing a touchdown pass to one of his ends and giving the Middies a 25-13 lead. They seemed well in command.

But the Mustangs had a world of speed, and the Navy defense couldn't cope with it. Two long touchdown runs turned the game around, and before you could say, "Raise the Jolly Roger," SMU led, 26-25.

Staubach went back to work. He circled the right end, stutter-stepping past tacklers. Then he was hit by three, four, five Mustangs. He didn't get up. The trainer came out and waved smelling salts under his nose. Minutes later he was standing over his center again, driving the team to the two-yard line, where they were stopped and forced to settle for a field goal. It was 28-26, with just 2:52 left, and the battered Staubach slumped on the bench, hoping his defense would do the rest.

They didn't. SMU rolled for 70 yards in just four plays and were suddenly on top, 32-28, with two minutes left. Navy got the kickoff back to the 40, but still had to go another 60 yards to win it.

In one of the most courageous drives ever seen, the Navy moved upfield under the proddings and personal heroics of its great quarterback. On the first play Roger romped around right end for 16 yards. Then he passed for 14 more. Setting up quickly, he cranked the arm and released. Complete! Another 12 yards. He dropped back again. This time his receivers were covered, so he took off right up the middle and bedazzled the SMU defenders for 15 yards. Now there were just two seconds left on the clock.

The huge Cotton Bowl crowd was hushed. The snap. Staubach dropped back. He fired into the end zone. There was receiver Ed Orr reaching for the ball. He had it . . . NO . . . he dropped it! The pass skittered off his fingertips. Navy had lost its first game of the year.

Though he'd never admit it, Staubach came out of the game a winner. Every adjective in the book was used to describe his performance. The game solidified his reputation as the most exciting performer in college football. He had everything it takes. If there was ever a question of his courage or his ability to play with pain, that, too, was eliminated.

Navy wasn't to lose another one all year, topping Notre Dame 35-14, and beating Dietzel and Army once more, 21-15. Roger was the star straight through. He finished the regular season with 107 of 161 passes for 1,474 yards and a .664 completion percentage. He was everybody's All-America and took every major award there was.

When he received the Heisman Trophy in New York a week after the Army game, Roger was asked the inevitable question for the first time. Did he plan to play pro ball?

"I can't really say for sure at this time whether I'll play pro ball," he answered. "I've still got a year and a half at Annapolis, then four years of Naval service to think about it. So I'm really concerned with my future in the Navy right now."

Staubach was only the fourth junior in football history to win the coveted Heisman Trophy, and that was just one of the factors that gave unbeaten and top-rated Texas a little more impetus in the 1964 Cotton Bowl game. That's right, the Middies got the bid by virtue of their fine 9-1 season. They were ranked right behind the Longhorns, and the game was billed as deciding the mythical National Championship.

Mighty Texas was just too much for the men of Annapolis. The game was won in the line, as the huge Texas tackles, ends, and linebackers stayed on Roger's back all day. He managed to pass for 228 yards, completing 21 of 31, but he couldn't take off on any of his patented scrambles. In fact, he was caught behind the line so often that he wound up with minus 47 yards rushing. The final score was 28-6. The Midshipmen were beaten decisively.

But nothing could take the luster off Roger's 1963 season. That was fortunate, because in 1964 his luck ran out. Before the season started, Wayne Hardin said his star would be better than ever. "He's more mature, older, and stronger," said Hardin, and few could argue with him off past performances. Navy lost some key men through graduation, but there was no reason to believe that the Middies wouldn't have a formidable team again.

Then it happened, in the first quarter of the very first game against Penn State. Roger was sandwiched between two Penn State defenders and slammed to the ground. When he got up, all the muscles in his right leg from the calf to the thigh were torn. There was also damage to the Achilles' tendon. He wouldn't be one hundred per cent all year. Roger the Dodger had lost his trump card.

"Roger wasn't the only one," Hardin said. "We had key personnel out at one time or another all year. I thought we had the potential to be great and we ended up losers.

"I really felt bad about Roger. He couldn't walk or run right all season, but he hung in there. Anyone else might have called it a year, but he wanted to help the team all he could. As a consequence, whenever he did start healing, he'd get racked up all over again."

Hardin's lament tells the tale. The team never got started. It won its first two, then went into a tailspin, losing five of its next six while tying the other. Dietzel and his Army team turned the trick, 11-8, in the finale, and the Middies finished the 1964 season with a lack-luster 3-6-1 mark.

A look at Roger's statistics is very revealing. He missed one game entirely, played just a few minutes in two others, yet he threw the ball more than the season before, completing 119 of 204 passes for 1,131 yards and just four touchdowns. His passing percentage dropped to .583, but his .636 career average is still the best in NCAA history.

The big change was in his rushing totals. Scrambling was always a big part of Staubach's game, but the leg injuries severely limited him, explaining the increased passing. He was officially credited with 104 carries for minus . . . yes, minus . . . one yard rushing.

There were so many superlatives used to describe Roger Staubach by the end of the 1963 season that most were used up now. He was the first sophomore in Naval Academy history to win the coveted Thompson Trophy, "awarded to the Midshipman who has done the most during the current year for the promotion of athletics at the Naval Academy." Then as a junior he won everything in sight, was named to every team in sight, and proclaimed the greatest collegiate football player in the land, maybe the best ever.

So after the injury-filled season of 1964, the questions became routine. What now, Rog? The pros, the Navy? Both, neither? Etc., Etc.

The facts were simple enough. Unless Roger got married, flunked his courses, or failed to pass his physical, he was committed to four years of service. He and Marianne were engaged, but wouldn't be married until after graduation. He wasn't about to flunk any courses, and his football injuries weren't so severe that he wouldn't pass the physical.

Roger spiced up the speculation by signing an optional contract with the Dallas Cowboys. It was a three-year pact, covering the years 1969-1972. He wouldn't be eligible until then. When it meant was that if he decided to play pro ball in 1969, the contract would automatically go into effect. If he decided to remain in the Navy, it was voided. He even got some regular payments from the Cowboys. If he played, the money would be part of his bonus. If not, the Cowboys just lost it. That's how much they wanted him.

"Roger will make it if he wants to," said Wayne Hardin as a parting shot. "He matured a great deal at Navy. He was more aware of the game and reacted to situations much better his last year. He learned to wait more and execute the play, rather than just taking off and improvising immediately. His arm was getting stronger and stronger. I think he could have made it big in the pros right away."

But he left to fulfill his obligation. Goodbye, Roger! In his absence, the team that had drafted him went about the business of becoming a powerhouse. By 1966, the Cowboys were atop the Eastern Division of the NFL, and they have stayed there every year since. They had all-stars at every position and one of the league's better quarterbacks in Dandy Don Meredith. The name Staubach was all but forgotten.

Where was he? Well, first there was a year stateside, training as a supply officer.

"My first year away from the Academy, I missed football terribly," he said. "The whole thing: the competitiveness, the crowds, my teammates. It all seemed so far in the past."

Then it was off to Vietnam for a year, where there were other things to think about. One day he got a small package from the States. It was "The Duke," the official football of the National Football League. The Cowboys had sent it to him as a present. Tex Schramm and Tom Landry hadn't forgotten.

"When I have the time and some guys to play catch with, I throw the ball about 400 times a day," Lieutenant Staubach said. "I intend to stay in the best shape I can and then make a fair decision about my future."

In Vietnam, Roger was a freight terminal officer, in charge of unloading supplies. He had over 130 sailors, 61 Vietnamese, and two other officers under him. He wasn't involved in any direct action, but was once caught in a mortar barrage that killed one man and wounded three. One of the shells struck about 200 yards from the bunker that he was in.

From the war zone, he returned to Pensacola to finish his hitch. There he found himself playing football again, this time with the base team which had a schedule of nine small colleges and the Quantico Marines. He slowly started getting his old wheels back in shape.

When Roger was set to report to the Cowboys in 1969, there were three veteran quarterbacks ahead of him. Don Meredith was number one, and at age 31, he seemed to have another seven or eight years ahead of him. Then there was Craig Morton and Jerry Rhome, two youngsters from the same graduating class as Roger. Yet they had picked up valuable experience by playing in spots and learning on the sideline. Staubach would be number four.

Then things began happening. First Rhome was traded—the Cowboy brass felt Morton had the better future. Then there was a real shocker. Without warning, Don Meredith notified the Cowboys that he was retiring. He'd had it. Dallas had lost the NFL championship to Green Bay in the final seconds two years running. Then they were beaten in the divisional playoffs by Cleveland. Meredith had had enough. The fans booed him and the opposition pounded him. He opted for a broadcasting career. In a dramatic turn of events, Craig Morton was the number one Dallas quarterback and his alternate was the rookie Staubach. The untried rookie Staubach.

"I'm confident in myself," Roger said. "I know I won't be number one immediately, but I want to make the team and find out what I can do.

"I gave up a career when I left the Navy. That should prove my confidence. But I'll never look back and regret it. If I hadn't tried to play pro ball now I'd spend the rest of my life wondering if I could have."

It wasn't long before everyone in the Cowboy camp was aware of Staubach's dedication. He worked hard and studied hard, determined to make up for lost time and regain the skills quickly that had made him such a great star at Navy. When Roger said he could run the 40-yard dash faster than the 4.9 seconds he did at Navy, few doubted him. Said one member of the Cowboys' staff:

"If you want Roger to do 4.75, just put him in there with a guy who does 4.8. Then he'll do 4.75."

As for Roger, his sound football mind made it easy for him to pick up the complex Cowboy offense. The thing he worried about was reading defenses.

"That will be a problem, recognizing defenses so you can change the play at the line of scrimmage. It's something you just can't do without experience. I just hope I get the chance to pick up the experience."

The first chance he got would be an experience, all right, one he'd never forget. It took place in July of 1969, and was the Cowboys' first rookie game against the yearlings of the Oakland Raiders. The Raider defensive candidates must have taken a cue from their veterans. One Oakland writer tapped them "The Eleven Angry Kids," a parody of the nickname given the Raider varsity defensive unit. Anyway, the angry kids really did a job on Roger Staubach.

When he dropped back to pass, they were around him like flies, and he had to run for his life. That resulted in hurried and off-balance passes, or throws that missed the receiver completely. By contrast, the Oakland rookie signal-callers, Ken Stabler and Eldridge Dickey, looked like seasoned veterans and the young Raiders romped 33-0.

"My timing was way off," Roger said afterward. "I overthrew guys and did a lousy job, that's all. I wasn't confused. Their secondary was quick and their line tough. I just didn't do a good job."

Coach Landry defended his rookie. "Roger's going to be great," the coach said, "but right now his mind's cluttered with our offense. He's trying to learn everything at once. He knows now that he's going to be our number two quarterback, not three or four, so he's pressing a bit."

Although Roger completed just two of 14 passes for 21 yards, he ended up as the team's leading ground gainer with 74 yards on only five carries. That was encouraging. He hadn't lost his ability to scramble and run, so his legs were still with him. The arm was already strong, so the timing and poise would come.

Roger kept working, through training camp and into the exhibition season. But Craig Morton was inheriting the number one spot for the first time and needed the work, too. So it was Craig who saw the bulk of the playing time in the exhibitions. Meanwhile, Staubach kept learning.

"I know I can still scramble," he said, "but I'm learning to be a drop-back passer. That's what it takes to be a professional quarterback. I'd still like to release the ball a little faster, and I've got to get used to reading defenses."

Ray Renfro, who coached the Cowboy receivers, said that Staubach surprised the coaches with his accuracy on short passes and his power on long bombs.

"He throws it 40 or 50 yards on a line," Renfro said. When asked how long it would take for Staubach to be a starter, he replied, "It will probably be a year or two before he has the experience to be a top quarterback, but there's no doubt that he has all the physical tools to do it."

But the football has strange ways of bouncing sometimes. Shortly before the Cowboys' 1969 opener with the St. Louis Cardinals, Morton injured a finger. The word was he wouldn't be ready in time. The Cowboys' starting quarterback would be Roger Staubach.

"Coach Landry was really nervous before that first game," Roger recalls. "I don't think he liked rookie quarterbacks and he was really worried about how the team would do. I thought I'd break the ice, so I went up to him with a big smile on my face and said, 'Gee, coach . . . just think . . . only a year ago I was playing quarterback for the Pensacola Garhawks against Middle Tennessee. Now I'm starting against St. Louis.' Well, he just gave me a long look, turned, and walked away."

Landry needn't have worried. The game was in capable hands. With the coach sending the plays in from the bench, Staubach ran the club cautiously, but well. Sticking to basic football and relying on precision execution, Dallas methodically destroyed the Cardinals. Roger made few mistakes. He handed off smoothly and passed well. The Cowboy defense did the rest, stopping the Cards in their tracks, and when it ended Dallas was on top, 24-3.

It made a great Cinderella story for the press. Rookie Staubach, away from football for four years, starts the first NFL game he plays in and leads his team to a victory. In fact, he made it look easy, and some said he was going to take up right where he left off after the great season of 1963. Even Roger breathed a sigh of relief when it was over. His confidence was rewarded and he looked forward to seeing more action.

Unfortunately, Landry didn't feel the same way. He acknowledged that Roger had done a fantastic job in his first game, but quickly reaffirmed his intention to use Craig Morton as his quarterback. He stuck to his word. Roger didn't start another game all year, and Morton, despite a sore elbow that severely hampered his ability to throw, stayed at the helm right through another divisional playoff loss to the Browns.

When 1970 rolled around, Staubach was hoping for more playing time. He got it, but not much more. He started three games that year, only when Morton was below par, and the Cowboys won two of them. Roger threw 82 passes and completed 44 for 542 yards and two touchdowns. But he was sacked by defensive players 19 times and threw eight interceptions.

Despite this, he managed to gain 221 yards on 27 carries, an 8.2 average, and was the Cowboys' number four runner. That might have been the problem. Roger wasn't staying in the pocket and Landry didn't like it. He was scrambling, hurrying his tosses, and playing a helter-skelter game that didn't go in the pros. He was making costly mistakes in-between brilliant flashes. One of these days he was bound to put it together.

The 1970 season was another frustrating one for the team. They won their division with a 10-4 mark, then topped Detroit 5-0, and San Francisco 17-10, to get into the Super Bowl. It was the goal they'd always sought.

But they'd done it on defense. Morton was soundly booed by the fans and criticized in the press. His arm still wasn't right. When the Colts whipped the Cowboys in the super game, 16-13, it marked the fifth straight year the powerful Dallas team was in the playoffs but didn't make it to the title. The fans and press clamored for a change.

So did Staubach. He had served his apprenticeship. He was 29 years old and felt he was ready.

"I'm extremely hungry for a starting football job," he told reporters. "I think I can be a starter for seven or eight years, preferably at Dallas, but if not, then somewhere else. If things don't work out this year, I want to be traded. Coach Landry knows about my feelings. I've spoken with him about it."

Landry was his usual evasive self. "I'm not worried about my quarterback situation," he said. "Either one of them (Morton or Staubach) can do the job. So I don't feel I have to make a decision because right now I plan on alternating them. Neither is clearly ahead of the other."

But then in the next breath, he said, "If Roger can't beat out Morton this year, I'll probably trade him."

Still the coach wouldn't commit. The exhibition season started and Morton looked like the same quarterback he had been for the past two years. His arm just didn't seem right. Meanwhile, Staubach was moving the team. Staying in the pocket longer and picking out his receivers with care, Roger the Dodger looked good. He started and played against the Colts, picking apart the famous Baltimore zone defense by hitting 12 of 17 passes for 193 yards and two touchdowns as the Cowboys won, 27-14.

After five exhibitions, the two quarterbacks had played about the same amount of time. And the comparison was an interesting one. Staubach had thrown six touchdown passes, Morton just one. And Jolly Roger had just one pass picked off, while Craig had thrown four interceptions. Who would you start?

Still, when the team opened against Buffalo, Morton was at the helm. It didn't last long. In came Staubach. But then Morton returned. Then Staubach. It was obvious now that Landry was planning to alternate his two quarterbacks, the thing Roger not only dreaded, but felt was bad for the team.

The coach began switching them indiscriminately. Then patterns started to emerge. He would switch them at the end of each quarter; after a while he changed it to each series of downs. Morale on the team was low once again.

Finally, on October 31, against the Chicago Bears, Landry reached the epitome of his little game. He alternated Morton and Staubach on every play, having his quarterback bring the next call in from the bench. It was ludicrous. Dallas lost to a mediocre Chicago team, 23-19. With the season already at the halfway mark, the Cowboys had a record of just 4-3 and trailed the upstart Washington Redskins by two games. Landry finally realized that something had to be done.

It just didn't make sense. Dallas had one of the most powerful teams ever assembled. Its running backs, Duane Thomas, Calvin Hill, and Walt Garrison all combined speed and power; the ends, Bob Hayes and Lance Alworth, were an equally dynamic duo. The offensive line boasted several all-pro performers, and the Doomsday Defense was right up there with the league's best. Yet the team wasn't winning.

Landry finally made his decision, and to this day can't or won't say why he made it. But he called Roger Staubach and informed him that from then on, he'd be the one and only starting quarterback for the Cowboys.

The news came as a shock, but it was music to Jolly Roger's ears. This was what he'd been working and waiting for the past two and a half seasons. A chance. A real chance. And he wasn't about to blow it. Landry would still call the plays, sending them in with his tight ends, Billy Truax and Mike Ditka, whom he now alternated on every play. But Staubach would remain the man taking the snap.

Roger debuted on November 7th, against the Cardinals at St. Louis. It was nip and tuck all the way, but Dallas prevailed, 16-13. The new quarterback ran a cool, competent show. He wasn't sensational, but the team won and perhaps the Cowboy fortunes were turning around.

The next week Dallas returned home and their oft-disappointed fans watched them with skepticism. They didn't have to worry. The Cowboys won easily over Philadelphia, 20-7. The following week it was the defense's show. They blanked the Skins, and Staubach played another errorless game in putting 13 points on the board. The final was 13-0, and the Cowboys were again tied for the number one spot.

Staubach was improving. He was staying in the pocket, running only when he had to, but running so well that the defenses were always aware of the threat. He beat the Rams, 28-21; buried the Jets, 52-10; and rolled over the Giants 42-14, before ending the regular season with a 31-12 victory over the Cardinals.

Seven straight wins, and the Cowboys had finished with

an 11-3 mark and the NFC Eastern Division championship. Landry's move had paid dividends. Roger Staubach started seven times and was a winner seven times. And he didn't do it by luck.

He was a dominant figure and inspiring leader. Sure, the team had its share of superstars and many of them had had fine years, but few achieved the perfection that Roger had in so short a time.

When the final statistics were released, Jolly Roger was the leading passer in the entire National Football League. He had thrown the football 211 times, completing 126 for a .597 average. His passes gained 1,882 yards and were good for 15 touchdowns. In addition, he led the league with an .892 average gain per pass and had only four of his tosses intercepted. And even better than that, only one of his last 192 throws had been picked off. He was truly sensational.

It wasn't even that he stopped scrambling so much. He just learned to pick his spots. In fact, he picked them 41 times, gaining 343 yards, for an incredible 8.4 yards per carry. But even while Staubach's feats were being praised up and down the league, Dallas fans wouldn't be believers until the team proved itself in the playoffs. They'd failed too many times in the past for anyone to get excited now. Sure, Staubach was a revelation, all right, but winning the Super Bowl was the name of the game in Dallas, and that's all anyone wanted to know.

The first step in the ultimate quest wouldn't be easy. The Cowboys had to meet the mighty Vikings of Minnesota, a powerhouse team weak at maybe one position: quarterback.

That turned out to be the difference. Coach Bud Grant switched back and forth between Bob Lee, Gary Cuozzo, and Norm Snead, strangely reminiscent of the old days at Dallas. The three-man parlay didn't work, and the Dallas defense contained the Vikes all afternoon.

Staubach, in the meantime, was running his own show. He patiently engineered two long touchdown drives, and two more that resulted in field goals as Dallas won it, 20-12. Now it was on to phase two, the National Conference championship game with the San Francisco 49ers, a team that had gained the finals by tripping the Washington Redskins.

The 49ers were solid, but they would go only as far as their quarterback, John Brodie, would take them. In 1970, Brodie had a tremendous year and his club was expected to get into the Super Bowl. But San Francisco ran into the Dallas defense one Sunday, and its season ended right there. In 1971, Brodie wasn't as sharp. He was prone to interceptions and never really got in the good groove. Yet his team won its division and was once again on the brink of the big one.

The two teams played it cautiously. Brodie was having his problems finding receivers, and Staubach was following Landry's instructions from the bench. He engineered one touchdown drive and the Cowboys led, 7-3, at the half.

In the third period Dallas had the ball on its own 23, a third and seven situation. If Staubach didn't make it here, the 49ers could easily take control of the game. Billy Truax shuttled the play in from the bench and Roger brought his club to the line. He took the snap and dropped straight back to pass. He did it so nicely and he looked more like John Unitas or Y.A. Tittle than Fran Tarkenton. Scramblers just don't drop back that way.

He looked downfield. Then he saw a couple of 49er linesmen drawing a bead on him. Instinctively, he took off It might have been Army-Navy all over again, with Roger the Dodger under a full head of steam. He zigged to one side, then spun back to the other, avoiding two tacklers. He was still surrounded, so he began retreating . . . to the ten, to the five, to his own three-yard line.

It was the kind of thing that Wayne Hardin had learned to live with, but it still gave Tom Landry fits. Just when it looked as though Staubach was trapped, he escaped once more and started moving upfield, wagging his shoulders from side to side, a running style that makes it look as if he's faking when there's no one to fake. Suddenly he was back over the 15, then the 20. Just when it seemed he would keep running, Jolly Roger pulled up short of the line of scrimmage and heaved a pass to Truax for a gain of 17 yards.

The exhausted 49ers regrouped. But Staubach had taken the starch out of their sails. He quickly snapped his team together and completed an 80-yard drive for the Cowboys' second touchdown. The 14-3 triumph was a tribute to the Dallas defense and to the field generalship of Roger Staubach.

And now there was one. In two weeks, the Cowboys would be going to New Orleans—to the Super Bowl. All that stood between Dallas and the ultimate victory was the Miami Dolphins.

Miami, an expansion team of just six years standing, already was on the brink of football supremacy. They had a fine young quarterback, Bob Griese, who led the AFC in passing and ranked second only to Staubach in the entire NFL. Their running duo of Larry Csonka and Jim Kiick rivaled closely the Cowboys' ground game; and Paul Warfield was as good a receiver as anyone in the game. Defensively, the Dolphins could be had, but the youngsters and veteran middle linebacker Nick Buoniconti had shut out the tough Colts just two weeks earlier. It looked like a hard game all the way.

The Dolphin offense knew it would have a difficult time, but figured it would put points on the scoreboard. Many thought the game would be decided by the Miami defense. Could it stop the Dallas attack, or more precisely, could it contain Roger Staubach?

Super Bowl VI took place on January 16, at Tulane Stadium in New Orleans, on a beautiful, sunshine-filled day.

Both teams started slowly. Then, midway through the first period, Miami fullback Csonka fumbled and linebacker Chuck Howley recovered at the Dallas 46. It was Csonka's first fumble all year, and 12 plays later it led to a Mike Clark field goal. Dallas led, 3-0. Then in the second period, Dallas got the ball on the Miami 24 and started driving.

Staubach directed the team flawlessly. He handed off to Thomas and Garrison, and watched them cut back against the grain, trapping the speedy Buoniconti, and moving for good gains. Or he dropped back and dumped short swing passes to his backs and ends. He marched his team up the field, bit by bit, slowly taking the heart out of the Miami defense. With the ball on the seven, Roger dropped back, stayed in the pocket, and whipped a perfect pass to Alworth in the near corner of the end zone. Clark converted, and it was 10-0 game.

The Dolphins made one serious bid in the first half, and it ended with a Garo Yepremian 31-yard field goal to make the halftime score 10-3.

But the Cowboys were doing the job. The front four, George Andrie, Jethro Pugh, Bob Lilly, and Larry Cole, were stopping the vaunted Miami running attack cold. And the linebackers and tough defensive backfield had taken Warfield's favorite lanes away from him. When Griese tried a page from Staubach's scrambling book, he was hauled down by Lilly for a 29-yard loss. The Dolphins were clearly on the run.

In the third quarter, Dallas took it to the Dolphins again. Staubach led another drive, keeping the ball mostly on the ground. With the ball at the 45, Duane Thomas cut back off the right side for 23 yards and a first down at the Miami 22.

Then the Cowboys got fancy. Flanker Bob Hayes came steaming around on a reverse and carried it to the six. Two plays later Thomas went bulldozing into the end zone. Clark's kick made it 17-3, and the Cowboys were slowly edging closer and closer to that elusive championship.

Miami knew it had to move fast. Griese started his club driving. He had a third and four on his own 49 and dropped back to pass. The young Dolphin signal-caller threw in the direction of his halfback, Jim Kiick. But he'd done that twice before on third down and Chuck Howley was waiting. The veteran linebacker picked the ball off and returned it 41 yards to the Miami nine. Now Dallas could really put it away.

This time it took Roger three plays. A play-action fake and perfect pass to tight end Mike Ditka from seven yards out did the trick. It was Jolly Roger's second touchdown pass of the afternoon and upped the score to 24-3. Dallas would have had more. Larry Cole jumped on a Griese fumble on the Dallas 16, and Staubach quickly moved his club all the way upfield to the Miami 20. On fourth down, Landry called for a field goal, but it was a fake, and holder Dan Reeves ran to the 13 and a first down.

Landry had waited six years for this. He was having some fun. He called an end-around for Ditka and the veteran receiver rambled to the one. That's where Dallas finally turned it over. Calvin Hill fumbled and Miami recovered to end the drive. But it didn't matter any more, the damage was done.

In the end, Landry was carried off the field. It was a big moment for him and he flashed one of his infrequent smiles. The 24-3 score showed just who was the best team in pro football. The Cowboys left little doubt. They'd beaten three powerful clubs on the way to the greatest triumph in their history.

Who would have thought it ten games earlier, when

Dallas was just 4-3, and seemingly faltering? Then a young man named Staubach was given the quarterback job. The Cowboys hadn't lost since.

That's right. Ten straight wins . . . no losses. In fact, in his three years with the Cowboys, Staubach had a 16-1 record as a starter. You can't do much better than that.

His Super Bowl effort was typical. The one-time Navy lieutenant completed 12 of the 19 passes he attempted, for 119 yards and two scores. As usual, there were no interceptions. His club had gained a record 252 yards on the ground, so it's obvious how well Dallas mixed its plays and executed them. Staubach hadn't done it alone.

Yet big Ditka, who's seen the best of them play during his decade in the league, had this to say: "Roger's a great leader. He just doesn't quit. He does it by getting out there and doing it, without wasting words. He brought this team to life."

So it finally appeared that the Cowboys were Roger's team, that he was the leader, number one. He spent the off-season receiving the plaudits that go with being a Super Bowl hero. In 1972 Roger was ready to go again.

But in the third exhibition game he tried to run over Rams middle linebacker Marlin McKeever. *Bang!* There was one of those collisions that only pro footballers know. McKeever was knocked woozy, momentarily. But Roger had a separated right shoulder.

"The same thing that made him try to run over McKeever will be what brings him back," said Coach Landry.

But while Roger was recovering, Morton again became the number one QB and led the Cowboys into the playoffs. Roger was finally activated for the final few games, throwing only 20 passes and completing nine in the regular season. Then came the first playoff game against the San Francisco 49ers. The Cowboys trailed 28-16 with only 2:02 remaining, and Landry, on a hunch, switched from Morton to Staubach.

In a matter of seconds it was the old Jolly Roger, never better. He marched his club downfield and fired a 20-yard TD to Billy Parks. Then the club got the ball on an onsides kick, and Rog was back. He scrambled for good yardage a couple of times, then hit Ron Sellers with a 10-yard scoring pass. He had done it, pulled the game out of the fire in the greatest pressure comeback in Dallas history. The Cowboys won, 30-28, and went to the NFC title game.

That's where the rustiness showed through. Roger got the start and had a bad day. The Redskins won, 26-3, eliminating Dallas from Super Bowl competition.

"I'm going to devote next season to making up for this one," a disheartened Staubach said after the game.

He did. He won the number one job from Morton in pre-season and went on to have another great year, in fact, his first real full, start-to-finish, season. He got the Cowboys into the playoffs and finished as the top passer in the NFC.

He completed 179 of 286 for 2,428 yards and a 62.6 percentage. It was the old Staubach accuracy. He tied with Roman Gabriel for the most TD passes in the NFL, 23, and had just 15 of his tosses intercepted. Many members of the great Cowboys dynasty were aging, and it didn't really come as a surprise when the team lost to Minnesota, 27-10, in the NFL title game. But no one could fault Roger; he had come all the way back. People have a tough time saying anything bad about Roger Staubach.

Yet there was still plenty of football to be played. Roger was aware that the Cowboy team was changing. He also knew that he couldn't lie down and relax just because the club might not be a strong contender for a few years. Besides, he had great faith in the Dallas organization. As far as he was concerned, there was no reason the team couldn't continue to win.

During the off-season Roger always made it a point to stay in shape. "I work out six days a week," he said, "running, doing sit-ups, lifting weights, stuff like that. I probably do more than I have to but I'm kind of fanatical about it."

But things were different in the off-season of 1974. Roger checked into the hospital for a foot operation, which was pronounced successful. But it set Roger's training program back by almost two months. Then in the preseason, he broke a couple of ribs. So when the season opened, he wasn't really ready.

It didn't show in the opener, as the Cowboys blanked Atlanta, 24-0. Then the roof fell in, as the club lost to Philadelphia, the New York Giants, and the Vikings. A loss to St. Louis made it four straight and the powerful Cowboys were suddenly floundering at 1-4.

So was Roger. His timing was way off. In the first five games he had thrown 10 interceptions, and that wasn't the real Staubach. No way.

"It was a period of hell for us," admitted the Dodger. "We'd never even lost three in a row before, now we dropped four straight. We found out the hard way that we couldn't rest on our laurels. Something had to give."

Slowly, the team began to pull out of it. They avenged three of the losses by beating Philly, St. Louis, and the Giants, to even their record at 4-4. Roger was playing better and was still trying to figure out what went wrong.

"I was obviously pressing in those early games," he said. "That never happened to me before. If we had been winning I wouldn't have thought that much about it, but we were losing."

If nothing else, Roger was discovering another outstanding receiver, rookie Drew Pearson, and he began going to the speedy youngster more and more. But Coach

Landry still called the plays and told Roger to stay in the pocket, not to scramble as much.

Ironically, Roger was knocked out of the most exciting game of the year, the Cowboys' second encounter with the Redskins. A concussion sidelined Roger with Dallas trailing, 23-10. That's when little-used backup quarterback Clint Longley came on to throw two TD passes and bring home a 24-23 triumph.

But that wasn't enough. Dallas finished the year at 8-6 and failed to make the playoffs for the first time in years. Now the question was which way would the team go. Would they continue to disintegrate? Or could they turn it around in 1975?

That was a question for Roger, too. Statistically, he had better years. He was 190 of 360 for 2,552 yards and a 52.8 percentage. But he threw for just 11 TDs and had 15 passes picked off. But remember, ten of them came in the first five games.

"I've never been down when I didn't fight back," Roger said. "There are people who are saying I don't have the ability, but they're wrong. I have the ability to compete with anybody. This season just makes me more determined about what I want to accomplish in the future. The Cowboys are in a state of transition now, but we have the people to make the Super Bowl, even while we're in transition. Just remember that."

And before 1975 started, Roger was still talking like he meant it.

"I'm healthy now and looking forward to a good season, as a leader and a consistent quarterback. That's one thing a team needs to win. And everyone around here wants to win."

The so-called experts viewed the Cowboys with a skeptical eye. Gone were such longtime stalwarts as Calvin Hill, Walt Garrison, Chuck Howley, Bob Lilly, and Cornell Green. But there were new names, such as the aforementioned Pearson, Golden Richards, Ed "Too Tall" Jones, Harvey Martin, Randy White, and Preston Pearson. They were all primed and ready.

In the second game of the season, the Cowboys and Roger showed they were ready to operate under pressure. Time and again they came back against tough St. Louis to tie the game in regulation and then win it in sudden death overtime. Roger was magnificent, hitting on 23 of 34 passes for 307 yards and three scores. Some people said it was a fluke, but others saw the handwriting. Coach Landry had blended in a group of enthusiastic youngsters with his great veterans and it was working.

The key, of course, was still Staubach, and as the season moved on, Roger continued to prove he was all the way back. Once again he was exhibiting all the qualities of passing, running, and leading that had been so successful in the past.

The Cowboys also surprised opponents by using a "shotgun" formation part of the time. The shotgun is when the quarterback stands several yards behind the center and takes a direct pass. It's essentially a passing formation and saves the QB dropback time. Other teams tried it in the past, but it hadn't always worked. The Cowboys and Roger were making it work.

It seemed that Dallas was involved in close games almost every week. When they lost an overtime game to archrival Washington, 30-24, the season was half over and the Cowboys, Redskins, and Cards all had 5-2 records. It was a real horse race for the playoff spots.

The games were still close. Against Philadelphia Roger had to rally the Cowboys from a 17-10 deficit with four minutes left to a close 20-17 win. He was 27 for 49 in that one, for 314 yards. Against the Giants, Roger hit 13 of 22 for 213 yards, and he used his running game to advantage. The Cowboys won, 14-3. And Roger showed he could throw long. His two TD passes were a 54-yarder to Jean Fugett and a 62-yarder to Golden Richards.

With the season nearing its end there was another big game against the Skins. This time Roger and his teammates were unbeatable. They dominated from start to finish and won, 31-10. Though the Cards won the division, Dallas was in the playoffs as the wild card entry, the team with the best second-place record in the conference. At the beginning of the year, how many people would have bet on that?

Roger had an outstanding regular season. He was second to Fran Tarkenton in NFC passing, completing 198 of 348 for 2,666 yards and a 56.9 percentage. He had 17 TDs and threw 16 intercepts, but performed well in the clutch on every occasion.

He proved it again in the first playoff game with the Vikings. In a hard-fought contest the Cowboys trailed, 14-10, with less than two minutes left. The ball was at their own 15, some 85 yards from paydirt. It seemed impossible for them to pull it out. The Vikes were in a prevent defense, yielding short stuff but nothing more.

By the time the clock wound down to 44 seconds the Cowboys were only at their own 25 with a fourth-and-16 situation. It seemed hopeless. Roger dropped back for what might be his last pass of the season. He threw toward the sidelines at midfield where Drew Pearson made a fine catch before going out of bounds. Now the ball was at the 50 with 37 seconds left.

Roger then wasted a pass, then called the identical play to Pearson, but deep. The speedy receiver blew down the right side as Roger looked, pumped, threw. Both Pearson and defender Nate Wright went for the ball at the five. Somehow Pearson caught it as Wright fell, and then waltzed into the end zone with the winning score. It was indeed a miracle finish.

Now the Cowboys had to meet the powerful Rams in

the NFC title game. Ram coach Chuck Knox knew Staubach was the guy to fear.

"He's a triple-threat quarterback," said the Ram coach. "It isn't just the fact that he can run or pass. He's a complete quarterback who can do all three things. First, he can set and throw out of the pocket. Second, he can roll out on planned plays, and third, he can scramble and either throw accurately or run effectively if the run is there."

Knox had plenty to fear. In the title game, Roger and the Cowboys simply blew the Rams off the field. It was an upset, and what an upset. The final score was 37-7, as the Rams were never in the game. Roger threw four touchdown passes and was brilliant.

"If Staubach is right, he's unstoppable," said Ram defensive coach Ray Malavasi. "He was so hot against us I just can't forget it."

Now it was on to the Super Bowl. In 10 years of Super Bowl competition, the Cowboys were the first wild card team to get there. But they had a tough nut to crack, the defending Super Bowl champ Pittsburgh Steelers.

That's when the Cowboys ran out of miracles. In fact, the solid Steelers were the ones who did the impossible, mainly two unbelievable clutch catches by wide receiver Lynn Swann. That was the difference in a 21-17 Steeler win.

But the Cowboys hadn't embarrassed themselves. They showed that the team was for real, and ready to resume its place among NFL powerhouses. The team had done something very remarkable. It had been built without taking a nosedive. The brief falter lasted just one year.

In 1976 they proved once and for all that they were still a top club. They got off the mark fast, as did Roger. In fact, during the first several games he was completing more than 70 percent of his passes. Some thought he might have a record-breaking season. The club was sound in all departments on offense and defense, and looked like it had a good shot to revenge its Super Bowl loss.

By midseason the team had lost just one game and Roger was still threading the needle. Then it happened, the one thing that can hamper a potentially brilliant season. Roger cracked a bone in one of the fingers of his throwing hand. He missed just one game, then decided to play with it.

"An injury like that is worse than one that puts you on the shelf," said one NFL veteran. "You're not hurt badly enough to sit, but just enough where it affects your playing."

And a quarterback's throwing hand is about the worse place for this kind of injury. For if the QB alters his grip or throwing motion just the slightest bit, he can lose that fine edge. That's what happened to Roger. The Cowboys' all-around power kept them winning, but Roger's stats began to show the problem.

As the season drew to a close, the Cowboys rolled in with another divisional title. They had an 11-3 mark. And Roger also hung in there. In fact, in the clinching game against Philadelphia he was 22 for 29, a great show. But perhaps in the final game of the year against Washington he again showed his problem. He couldn't seem to hit his targets, even though his receivers were open. He couldn't seem to really control his passes. He threw two intercepts, the second leading to the insurance score for the Skins.

When it ended, Washington had a 27-14 victory, and Roger had completed just five of 22 passes. That certainly wasn't the real Staubach. For the year he was 208 for 369 for a 56.4 percentage and 2,715 yards. He threw for 14 TDs and had 11 picked off. A good year, but not a great one for him. Though the Cowboys were a powerhouse, they couldn't do it without the accurate arm of their quarterback.

In the first round of the playoffs the Cowboys would

meet the Rams, the team they buried the year before. But that was when Roger was firing bull's-eyes. This day he wasn't. He was overthrowing his receivers right from the start. Without the passing threat, the tough Rams defense keyed on the run and stopped the Cowboy attack. The Dallas defense fought well, but it wasn't quite enough. When it ended the Rams had a 14-12 victory, and for Dallas it was wait till next year.

Although Roger is in his mid-thirties, he has always kept himself in top shape and expects to be around for another few years. If he stays healthy, there's no doubt that he'll take up where he left off at the beginning of the '76 season. His supporting cast is that good. And to many, Roger Staubach remains the epitome of what a pro quarterback should be.

He's a devoted human being, devoted to God, his family, and his country. He believes in all the fine principles under which this country was founded. He's an honorable man who won't compromise his own ethics for anything. Yet he has survived and surfaced as a superstar in one of the toughest businesses in the world.

Yes, Tex Schramm made a wise draft choice back in 1964. He said then that the Cowboys were willing to wait, willing to gamble on greatness. They waited all right—and they got themselves a leader and a winner. He was worth waiting for.

As usual, the Jolly Roger is once again flying high.

# ★ STATISTICS ★

## Ken Stabler

| Year | Team | Att. | Comp. | Pct. | Yds. | TD | Int. | Ave. Gain |
|------|------|------|-------|------|------|----|------|-----------|
| 1970 | Oak. | 7 | 2 | 28.6 | 52 | 0 | 1 | 7.43 |
| 1971 | Oak. | 48 | 24 | 50.0 | 268 | 1 | 4 | 5.58 |
| 1972 | Oak. | 74 | 44 | 59.5 | 524 | 4 | 3 | 7.08 |
| 1973 | Oak. | 260 | 163 | 62.7 | 1,997 | 14 | 10 | 7.68 |
| 1974 | Oak. | 310 | 178 | 57.4 | 2,469 | 26 | 12 | 7.96 |
| 1975 | Oak. | 293 | 171 | 58.4 | 2,296 | 16 | 24 | 7.84 |
| 1976 | Oak. | 291 | 194 | 66.7 | 2,737 | 27 | 17 | 9.40 |
| Totals | | 1,283 | 776 | 60.5 | 10,343 | 88 | 71 | 8.06 |

## Billy Kilmer

| Year | Team | Att. | Comp. | Pct. | Yds. | TD | Int. | Ave. Gain |
|------|------|------|-------|------|------|----|------|-----------|
| 1961 | S.F. | 34 | 19 | 55.9 | 286 | 0 | 4 | 8.41 |
| 1962 | S.F. | 13 | 8 | 61.5 | 191 | 1 | 3 | 14.69 |
| 1963 | S.F. | DID NOT PLAY | | | | | | |
| 1964 | S.F. | 14 | 8 | 57.1 | 92 | 1 | 1 | 6.57 |
| 1965 | S.F. | DID NOT PLAY | | | | | | |
| 1966 | S.F. | 16 | 5 | 31.3 | 84 | 0 | 1 | 5.25 |
| 1967 | N.O. | 204 | 97 | 47.5 | 1,341 | 6 | 11 | 6.57 |
| 1968 | N.O. | 315 | 167 | 53.0 | 2,060 | 15 | 17 | 6.54 |
| 1969 | N.O. | 360 | 193 | 53.6 | 2,532 | 20 | 17 | 7.03 |
| 1970 | N.O. | 237 | 135 | 57.0 | 1,557 | 6 | 17 | 6.57 |
| 1971 | Wash. | 306 | 166 | 54.2 | 2,221 | 13 | 13 | 7.26 |
| 1972 | Wash. | 225 | 120 | 53.3 | 1,648 | 19 | 11 | 7.32 |
| 1973 | Wash. | 227 | 122 | 53.7 | 1,656 | 14 | 9 | 7.29 |
| 1974 | Wash. | 234 | 137 | 58.5 | 1,632 | 10 | 6 | 6.97 |
| 1975 | Wash. | 346 | 178 | 51.4 | 2,440 | 23 | 16 | 7.05 |
| 1976 | Wash. | 206 | 108 | 52.4 | 1,252 | 12 | 10 | 6.08 |
| Totals | | 2,737 | 1,463 | 53.4 | 18,992 | 140 | 136 | 6.94 |

## Terry Bradshaw

| Year | Team | Att. | Comp. | Pct. | Yds. | TD | Int. | Ave. Gain |
|------|------|------|-------|------|------|----|------|-----------|
| 1970 | Pitt. | 218 | 83 | 38.1 | 1,410 | 6 | 24 | 6.47 |
| 1971 | Pitt. | 373 | 203 | 54.4 | 2,259 | 13 | 22 | 6.06 |
| 1972 | Pitt. | 308 | 147 | 47.7 | 1,884 | 12 | 12 | 6.12 |
| 1973 | Pitt. | 180 | 89 | 49.4 | 1,183 | 10 | 15 | 6.57 |
| 1974 | Pitt. | 148 | 67 | 45.3 | 785 | 7 | 8 | 5.30 |
| 1975 | Pitt. | 286 | 165 | 57.7 | 2,055 | 18 | 9 | 7.18 |
| 1976 | Pitt. | 192 | 92 | 47.9 | 1,177 | 10 | 9 | 6.13 |
| Totals | | 1,705 | 846 | 49.6 | 10,756 | 76 | 99 | 6.31 |

## Roger Staubach

| Year | Team | Att. | Comp. | Pct. | Yds. | TD | Int. | Ave. Gain |
|------|------|------|-------|------|------|----|------|-----------|
| 1969 | Dallas | 47 | 23 | 48.9 | 421 | 1 | 2 | 8.96 |
| 1970 | Dallas | 82 | 44 | 53.7 | 542 | 2 | 8 | 6.61 |
| 1971 | Dallas | 211 | 126 | 59.7 | 1,882 | 15 | 4 | 8.92 |
| 1972 | Dallas | 20 | 9 | 45.0 | 98 | 0 | 2 | 4.90 |
| 1973 | Dallas | 286 | 179 | 62.6 | 2,428 | 23 | 15 | 8.49 |
| 1974 | Dallas | 360 | 190 | 52.8 | 2,552 | 11 | 15 | 7.09 |
| 1975 | Dallas | 348 | 198 | 56.9 | 2,666 | 17 | 16 | 7.66 |
| 1976 | Dallas | 369 | 208 | 56.4 | 2,715 | 14 | 11 | 7.36 |
| Totals | | 1,723 | 977 | 56.7 | 13,304 | 83 | 73 | 7.72 |